CONTENTS

SPLITTING *UP*

A GUIDE TO SEPARATION AND DIVORCE IN SCOTLAND

DAVID NICHOLS

M.A., Ph.D.
Writer to the Signet

Published by
The Scottish Association of Citizens Advice Bureaux
82 Nicolson Street
Edinburgh
EH8 9EW.

ISBN 0 905831 05 5

INTRODUCTION

THINKING THINGS OVER

This book is about splitting up — you and your partner separating or getting divorced. It is a very stressful experience with serious emotional and financial consequences. Not only have you to adjust to living without your former partner, but there are a host of practical matters which you will have to think about — such as where to stay, who is to look after the children, how to get enough money to live on, how splitting up will affect your tax and social security position. These are dealt with in detail in the following chapters.

It is worthwhile thinking about all of these things before you decide to leave your partner because once the process of splitting up has started it is very difficult to stop it. Don't rush into making a decision you might later regret.

Many problems in a relationship are due to a lack of communication between partners or a misunderstanding of the other's needs and desires. You may find that talking things over with your partner or consulting one of the organisations listed below resolves the problems between you. On the other hand, your relationship may have deteriorated to such an extent that reconciliation is impossible and splitting up is the only sensible answer. Even in this case talking things over with your partner may help in arriving at mutually agreeable solutions to the problems each of you will face in the future.

Think about consulting your (and perhaps even your partner's) family before making a decision. They may be able to help sort out the difficulties in your relationship and can be a source of emotional and practical support if you and your partner decide to split up. Another source of help is friends - particularly those who have been through the process of splitting up themselves.

While only you and your partner can decide whether to continue living together or to split up, others will be affected by the decision and you should bear their interests in mind. Any children will obviously be very much affected, but staying together for the sake of the children is not necessarily the right answer. It may be better for them to be upset for a short period, but grow up in a home free of tension. Your and your partner's parents will also be concerned about keeping in touch with their grandchildren.

There are many organisations offering information, advice and counselling services for people considering splitting up.

- Citizens Advice Bureaux
- Marriage Counsellors
- Scottish Family Conciliation Service
- Women's Aid
- Shelter
- Scottish Council for Single Parents
- Council Housing Departments
- DHSS
- Gingerbread

A Citizens Advice Bureau offers free confidential advice, help and information. It is probably the best general source of help. Many bureaux offer free legal advice sessions as well. There are over 70 Citizens Advice Bureaux in Scotland. Their telephone numbers and addresses are in local telephone directories. Information about your nearest bureau can be obtained from:

Marriage counsellors provide a confidential service for people who are having difficulty in their marriage or other personal relationships. You can obtain help even if you are definitely thinking of splitting up and you will not be advised to seek a reconciliation or make your relationship work whatever the cost. There are 17 Marriage Guidance Councils throughout Scotland and over 50 centres where trained marriage counsellors can be seen. Interviews are usually by appointment. You can find out the address of your local branch from a telephone directory, or local Citizens Advice Bureau or:

There are also a number of Marriage Guidance Advisory centres for Catholics in different parts of Scotland which offer help on all aspects of family life. Further information can be obtained from:

ORGANISATIONS WHICH CAN HELP

CITIZENS ADVICE BUREAUX

Scottish Association of Citizens Advice Bureaux
82 Nicolson Street
Edinburgh EH8 9EW.
Telephone 031-667 0156/7/8.

MARRIAGE COUNSELLORS

The Scottish Marriage Guidance Council
26 Frederick Street
Edinburgh EH2 2JR
Telephone 031-225 5006.

Catholic Marriage Advisory Council
18 Park Circus
Glasgow
Telephone 041-332 4914.

These offer assistance to couples and their families who are splitting up, whether or not they are married. The conciliator interviews you and your partner, usually together but sometimes separately, to enable you both to reach an agreement on all matters concerning the breakdown of your relationship, particularly those involving the children. You can either contact the service directly yourself or ask your solicitor to refer you. Your local Citizens Advice Bureau will tell you if there is a service in your area. At the time of writing, Strathclyde, Central and Lothian regions are covered. More information from :

SCOTTISH FAMILY CONCILIATION SERVICES

Scottish Family Conciliation Service (Lothian)
127 Rose Street South Lane
Edinburgh EH2 5BB.
Telephone 031-226 4507.

Women's Aid run refuges or safe houses for abused women and their children which provide a safe place for you to stay in while you decide what to do next. Women's Aid also provide useful information including advice on your legal rights, housing options and emotional support. They operate on a 24 hour basis. To contact your nearest Women's Aid Group look in the telephone directory or contact your local Citizens Advice Bureau or:

WOMENS' AID

Scottish Women's Aid
11 St Colme Street
Edinburgh EH3 6AA.
Telephone 031-225 8011 (24 hour service).

Shelter offers help and information about housing and can be contacted at :

SHELTER
65 Cockburn Street
Edinburgh.
Telephone 031-226 6347.

SCOTTISH COUNCIL FOR SINGLE PARENTS

It gives advice and information to single parents or those helping them. They also keep information on independent self-help groups for single parents throughout Scotland. They can be contacted at:

13 Gayfield Square
Edinburgh.
Telephone 031-556 3899.
or 39 Hope Street
Glasgow.
Telephone 041-221 1681.

COUNCIL HOUSING DEPARTMENTS

Your local district (or islands) council housing department can give you advice on getting another house, housing benefit, and, if you and/or your partner are already in one of their houses, having the tenancy transferred to you and your liability for rent arrears.

DHSS

The Department runs a confidential service giving advice on benefits which would be available on splitting up. Dial 100 and ask for Freefone DHSS.

GINGERBREAD

This is a self-help organisation for one-parent families. Your local Citizens Advice Bureau will be able to tell you if there is a group in your area, or contact :

Scottish Gingerbread Office,
39 Hope Street
Glasgow.
Telephone 041-248 6840.

OTHER SOURCES OF HELP

People or organisations you could turn to for help include your church, doctor, health visitor, the Samaritans, and your local social work department. Support for people with problems is thinnest on the ground in rural areas, but you may find that your local Council of Voluntary Service can assist you. Appendix 4 contains a list of publications which you might find helpful.

SOLICITORS

DO I NEED A SOLICITOR?

You will generally need the services of a solicitor if you decide to split up. You may need to get a court order or formal agreement for maintenance for yourself and any children. Or you and your partner may need to sell your home and buy other accommodation. Or you may need to go to court about custody of the children and rights to visit them. Finally, you will generally need to use a solicitor if you want to start divorce proceedings.

You should think about consulting a solicitor before deciding whether to split up. He or she can advise you about your legal rights on a number of issues (such as occupancy of the family home or custody of the children). This information will put you in a better position to talk things over and reach an agreement with your partner. See Appendix 3 for how to find a solicitor.

LEGAL AID

If you cannot afford to pay for a solicitor yourself you can be helped through three different schemes:
- The fixed fee interview scheme — for an initial explanatory interview.
- Legal advice and assistance — for advice and pre-court work.
- Legal aid — for court work.

A list of those solicitors who take part in these schemes can be obtained from your local Legal Aid Committee (address in the telephone book), Citizens Advice Bureau or Sheriff Court. Further details of these three legal aid schemes are given in Appendix 1.

EMERGENCY SITUATIONS

This chapter tells you how to deal with situations where you must act quickly in order to get the help you need.

DEALING WITH VIOLENT OR THREATENING BEHAVIOUR

INFORMAL METHODS
INVOLVING THE POLICE
TELLING YOUR PARTNER TO LEAVE
GETTING AN INTERDICT FROM THE COURT
GETTING AN EXCLUSION ORDER FROM THE COURT

WHAT TO DO IF YOUR PARTNER PUTS YOU OUT

EMERGENCY ACCOMMODATION

PROTECTING THE CHILDREN

CHILDREN BEING TAKEN ELSEWHERE IN THE U.K.
CHILDREN BEING TAKEN OUT OF THE U.K.

GETTING MONEY

PROTECTING YOUR MONEY

*YOUR PARTNER
TRIES TO SELL THE
HOME OR GIVE UP
THE TENANCY*

*YOUR PARTNER
STOPS PAYING FOR
THE HOME*

*SAFEGUARDING
YOUR BELONGINGS*

*PREVENTING YOUR
PARTNER FROM
REMOVING BASIC
FURNITURE*

Your partner may assault you, threaten you or otherwise make your life so unpleasant that you have to leave home. Since the victim of violent or threatening behaviour is normally a woman, the sections dealing with these topics are written on this basis. But the advice applies equally to a man subjected to such treatment. You can :

- try to stop it informally; OR
- call the police; OR
- if you are the sole owner or tenant and you and your partner are not married to each other, tell him to leave; OR
- obtain an interdict prohibiting your partner from behaving in that way; OR
- get a court order excluding your partner from the home.

*DEALING WITH
VIOLENT OR
THREATENING
BEHAVIOUR*

INFORMAL METHODS

If the violent or threatening behaviour has only just begun you may be able to get your partner to stop it without having to take legal proceedings. You could talk it over with him and say that unless the violence or threats stop you will call the police or go to court. You may find it helpful to involve a friend or relative or counselling agencies like Marriage Guidance or Women's Aid if you do not feel like tackling your partner directly.

Another approach is to get your solicitor to write a warning letter to your partner. This may prove effective as it will make it clear that you are seriously considering further action unless things improve.

It is unlikely that talking things over will help if your partner has been maltreating you for some time. In these cases you will need to take legal proceedings to protect yourself. It may be advisable to stay away from home (in a Women's Aid refuge for example) to avoid further violence while the court action is in progress.

INVOLVING THE POLICE

Physical assaults and threats of violence are criminal offences even when they take place in the home. The fact that the offender and victim are married or cohabiting makes no difference. An offence may be committed even if there is no actual or threatened violence. For instance creating a noisy scene can amount to a breach of the peace. It can also be an offence for your partner to harass you in order to get you to leave if you are entitled to live in the home.

You can call the police if you are assaulted, threatened or there is a scene. The main advantage of the police is that they are available at any time of the day or night. But for a variety of reasons they are reluctant to become involved in what they see as domestic disputes. The police will not normally arrest your partner unless your version of the incident is corroborated in some way. Corroboration does not mean that there has to be another eye-witness to the incident. Your injuries, signs of a struggle about the home or screams and shouts heard by neighbours could be sufficient.

If the police arrest your partner this may only be a short-term solution. He will usually be kept in custody overnight and be released the next morning after a brief appearance in court. His trial will be held later and you will be required to give evidence if he pleads not guilty. If your partner is found guilty he will normally be fined. Imprisonment is usually only imposed for serious or repeated assaults. Being arrested, tried and sentenced will not necessarily stop your partner from repeating his violent behaviour when he returns home. On the other hand an appearance in court may deter an otherwise law abiding man, and a conviction will be useful if you decide to apply for an exclusion order later.

When no arrest is made the police will attempt to calm things down. They may warn your partner that if the conduct occurs again he will be arrested.

You can complain, either personally or through a solicitor, to the Chief Constable or the Procurator fiscal if you think the police did not take the appropriate action in response to your call. However this is unlikely to produce a favourable result. You could also let your local Women's Aid group or similar organisation know of your experience; they may be prepared to approach the police if they receive similar complaints from several people.

TELLING YOUR PARTNER TO LEAVE

If you are the sole owner or tenant and you and your partner are not married to each other, you can simply tell him to leave. Unless your partner has previously been granted occupancy rights (see p 24) by the court he has no right to remain in the home once you have told him to leave. It is not clear whether you are legally obliged to give your partner a reasonable time to move out. But you are unlikely to face legal proceedings if you allow your partner a few days (or less if he has been violent) to remove his belongings and find alternative accommodation. If your partner refuses to leave, you can either change the locks on the door or apply to the court for an order requiring him to leave. Once this order has been granted, sheriff officers can be instructed to remove your partner and his belongings from the home, by force if necessary. It may be a good idea to move out until your partner has gone.

You can only take this course of action where your partner has no occupancy rights. If he has occupancy rights because he is a (joint) owner or tenant, or is married to you, or has been granted occupancy rights by a court order, you will have to go to court for an exclusion order (see p 28) or recall of the occupancy rights granted to get him out.

GETTING AN INTERDICT FROM THE COURT

An interdict is a court order prohibiting the person named in it from doing certain acts specified in the order or being in a specified area, such as the home or stair. You can obtain an interdict prohibiting your partner from assaulting, threatening or molesting you. You can apply for an interdict whether you and your partner are married or cohabiting or living together or apart.

If you are married you can get a special kind of interdict against your husband called a matrimonial interdict. The main advantage of this is that a power of arrest can be attached to it (see below).

If you are not married you can still get an interdict, but you can only get a matrimonial interdict if you and your partner are joint owners or tenants or the court has granted one of you occupancy rights.

A solicitor's help is needed to obtain an interdict from the court - usually the local sheriff court. The court will usually grant you an interdict against violence or molestation fairly readily, especially if you can show you have been ill-treated before.

As soon as your application has been lodged in court you can ask the court to grant an INTERIM INTERDICT. This will give you immediate protection and will last until your interdict application is heard (generally in a week or so). An interim interdict is usually granted without notice of your application being given to your partner. But if you want a power of arrest to be attached to it, your partner has to be given an opportunity to put his case to the court first.

If your partner knowingly does what the interdict prohibits he is said to have breached the interdict. With the help of your solicitor you can report the breach to the court. Breach of interdict is punishable by a fine or imprisonment, but a warning is often given to a first offender.

Where your interdict has a POWER OF ARREST attached to it the police can arrest your partner without a warrant if they suspect him of having breached the interdict - by assaulting you or loitering on the stair for example. A power of arrest may make the police readier to take positive action in response to your call. However, the police only have a power to arrest; they do not have to use this power in every case and may not do so in yours. You can complain, either personally or through your solicitor, to the Chief Constable or the Procurator fiscal if you think the police should have arrested your partner.

If your partner is arrested for breach of a matrimonial interdict he will be taken to the police station. The police will then either release him or if further violence seems likely, keep him in custody until he is brought before the court - usually the next morning. If your partner is kept in custody but the

Procurator fiscal decides not to take criminal proceedings, the fiscal will apply to the sheriff for your partner to be kept in custody for a further two days. The sheriff will grant this application if satisfied that there was a breach of interdict which you are going to report to the court and that there is a substantial risk of further violence.

Even if the police do not arrest your partner or they arrest and then release him, you can still report the breach of interdict to the court.

GETTING AN EXCLUSION ORDER FROM THE COURT

An exclusion order is a court order which suspends your partner's right to occupy the home. It is granted along with orders to remove him from the home — by force if necessary — and to prevent him returning without your permission.

It will usually take a few months before your application for an exclusion order is heard, as it is almost certain to be opposed by your partner. In the meantime you can apply for an INTERIM EXCLUSION ORDER to exclude your partner until the case is heard. An interim exclusion order will not be granted unless your partner has been given an opportunity to challenge it. Before it grants an interim exclusion order or an exclusion order the court must be satisfied that the order is necessary to protect you or your children from any conduct (or threatened or reasonably apprehended conduct) by your partner which injures or could injure your physical or mental health or that of your children. Even where you can show this the court still looks at all the circumstances of the case to make sure that your partner's exclusion would be reasonable. For further information see p 28 .

WHAT TO DO IF YOUR PARTNER PUTS YOU OUT

If your partner throws you out or changes the locks on the door so you cannot get in, you could try to talk to him directly, or through a friend or relative, to see if you can return at least on a temporary basis. It may be a good idea to wait a few hours to allow tempers to cool.

Alternatively, you can: —

BREAK IN. This is not advisable unless you are an owner or tenant and you can do it without causing a breach of the peace.
CALL THE POLICE. Although the police can arrest your partner they

are more likely to persuade him to let you back into the house by pointing out that putting you out is a criminal offence. The police may be more willing to take action if you are a (joint) owner or tenant than if you merely have occupancy rights.

There is only one situation where your partner does not commit an offence by putting you out. This is where :
● you and your partner are not married to each other; AND
● you are not a (joint) owner or tenant or the court has not granted you occupancy rights; AND
● you have been asked to move out and refused to do so.
Even in this case the police may try to persuade your partner to let you back in temporarily if you have nowhere else to go, and they may help you collect your belongings. If you want to live in the house you will have to apply to the court for occupancy rights (see p 24).

APPLY TO THE COURT FOR AN ORDER RE-INSTATING YOU. If you are a (joint) owner or tenant the court will order your partner to let you back into the home, unless your partner can satisfy the court that your behaviour was so bad (violence or heavy drinking for example) that you should be kept out. If you have only occupancy rights (that is you are not a (joint) owner or tenant) the court looks at all circumstances of the case before deciding whether or not it is reasonable that you should be allowed to return.

If you have nowhere else to live, or if the children need you to look after them, your application is likely to be granted. You should apply to the court at once as delay will weaken your case. You can also ask the court, in the event of its ordering your partner to allow you back in, to interdict (prohibit) your partner from putting you out, or threatening to put you out again.

If you and your partner are not married to each other and you are not a (joint) owner or tenant, you will have to apply to the court for occupancy rights (see p 24). Once the court has granted these you can apply for an order re-instating you, and your partner can be interdicted from shutting you out again. You should not delay in applying for occupancy rights as the court will only grant your application if you are living in the home, or have recently been living there.

CLAIM COMPENSATION. You can apply to the court for an order requiring your partner to pay you money as compensation for the cost of finding alternative accommodation and for the loss of your right to occupy the home. In practice this remedy is not much use because most people who throw their partners out are not worth suing. You cannot claim compensation if you are not a (joint) owner or tenant, or you did not have occupancy rights before you were put out.

EMERGENCY ACCOMMODATION

The sort of accommodation available to you may depend on whether you are on your own or have the children with you and how long you are likely to be there for.
The choices are:

FRIENDS OR RELATIONS.

LOCAL AUTHORITY OR HOUSING ASSOCIATION ACCOMMODATION. Sometimes these bodies have houses which are available for letting to people on a short term basis. Ask your district council housing department, a New Town Development Corporation or a housing association in your area. If you are homeless and are a priority case your local district or islands council has an obligation to provide you (and your children) with temporary accommodation while they are making enquiries into your case (see p 31 for further details and provision of permanent accommodation).

WOMEN'S AID REFUGES. These are houses run by Women's Aid but are not available in every part of Scotland. (see p 3 for how to contact Women's Aid).

PRIVATE RENTED PROPERTY. Furnished flats or houses are available through estate or accommodation agencies or advertisements in newspapers or local newsagents. This sort of accommodation can be expensive but you can claim Housing Benefit (see p 64) to help pay the rent. Single Payments from the DHSS may be available to pay rent in advance or a returnable deposit.

HOTELS OR BED AND BREAKFAST. This type of accommodation is not suitable for children and the DHSS may not pay the full cost.

PROTECTING THE CHILDREN

If you think your partner is likely to remove the children from your care in order to take them to live with him or her, or less commonly to take them abroad, you can apply to the court for :

- an interdict prohibiting removal of the children from your care and control; OR
- an interdict prohibiting removal of the children from Scotland. You can apply for this interdict even though the children are living in Scotland with your partner.

If the children are living with you it would be a good idea to apply for sole custody of them at the same time if you have not already done so.

Delay in applying for an interdict may be fatal if the children are about to be taken abroad. In urgent cases an interdict can be obtained at any hour of the day or night.

CHILDREN BEING TAKEN ELSEWHERE IN THE U.K.

Your husband or wife does not commit a criminal offence by taking the children away from you unless force was used or the children are to be taken abroad (see p 15). An unmarried father does however commit an offence unless he has been awarded custody of the children. If no criminal offence has been committed the police will not intervene and you should see your solicitor.

Contact your solicitor promptly if your partner takes the children away from you in breach of an interdict prohibiting this or an order giving you sole custody. Your solicitor will arrange for the matter to be reported to the court. The court will order your partner to return the children and, if an interdict was breached, punish him or her for contempt. This takes the form of a fine or imprisonment, although a warning is normally given for a first offence. If your partner fails to return the children, sheriff officers can be called in to search for them and hand them back to you.

If the children have been taken to another part of the U.K., your solicitor will arrange for the appropriate action to be taken there to recover them.

If you did not have an interdict or sole custody you will have to apply to the court for custody in order to get the children back.

Your partner commits a criminal offence by taking or attempting to take the children out of the U.K. without your consent if you have a custody order or interdict prohibiting their removal from your care and control or from Scotland. Your partner is liable to be fined or imprisoned and can be extradited from many countries to stand trial in Scotland. Sheriff officers and the police can be asked to assist in tracing the children and preventing their removal out of the country.

You can also request the Passport Office in Glasgow not to issue a passport for the children without your consent, but the children may already have passports or be on your partner's passport. The police can be asked to place the children on a "stop list" and alert the immigration authorities at all airports and seaports. If the children are detected their emigration will be prevented. The "stop list" should only be used if there is a real risk of removal; you should not use it merely as a precautionary measure.

Once the children are out of the U.K. it can be hard to recover them. It may be difficult to trace them, you may have to contest custody in the other country's courts and legal aid may not be available. But some countries (mainly European but also Canada) have signed international conventions on child abduction and custody. More countries will probably sign later. If your children have been taken to one of these countries the authorities in Scotland will contact the authorities there who will endeavour to trace them and if successful will arrange for your rights of custody to be recognised and enforced. Your solicitor will advise you on what action to take.

If you and/or the children are left without any money you may be able to get money from :

> THE DHSS. You can claim Supplementary Benefit for yourself and any children if you are not working (see p 62 for further details). An immediate payment may be made at your local office if you have been left without money. Outwith office hours (at the weekend, for example) you should contact the police or local social work department who will put you in touch with the social security emergency service. An official will visit you, and, if satisfied that your claim is genuine, will give you sufficient cash to tide you over until you can claim benefit. If you are working you may be able to claim Family Income Supplement and One Parent Benefit (see p 64 and 65).

CHILDREN BEING TAKEN OUT OF THE U.K.

GETTING MONEY

YOUR LOCAL SOCIAL WORK DEPARTMENT. They may be able to help if the DHSS can't.

YOUR PARTNER. You can apply to the court for an order requiring your husband or wife to pay aliment for you. Your cohabiting partner may also be ordered to pay aliment for the children but not for you. Once your application is lodged you can ask the court to award a weekly amount called INTERIM ALIMENT. This interim aliment lasts until your application for aliment is heard. You can use this method if you know your partner's whereabouts and he or she has the means to pay.

LOANS. Your bank may allow you to overdraw your account but you will have to satisfy them that you will be able to pay it back eventually. Your friends and family may be prepared to lend you money, but again you should think about how you are going to repay them. Do not borrow from money lenders if you can possibly avoid it. Their rates of interest are very high and the other terms of the loan may be unfavourable.

SELLING OR PAWNING YOUR BELONGINGS. The drawback is that it will cost you a lot more to replace them later on. It is a criminal offence to sell your partner's belongings or items which you both own without permission. See p 34 for what is likely to be jointly owned.

PROTECTING YOUR MONEY

If you have a joint account with your partner there is a danger that your partner will withdraw all the money from it. You can prevent this by:—

- withdrawing all or part of the money yourself, OR
- contacting the bank or building society. Some organisations will then not allow withdrawals to be made unless both you and your partner sign the withdrawal form.

YOUR PARTNER TRIES TO SELL THE HOME OR GIVE UP THE TENANCY

Your partner may try to sell the home or give up the tenancy. The way in which you are protected against this depends on whether you are a (joint) owner or tenant and whether you and your partner are married to each other.

YOUR PARTNER IS THE SOLE OWNER OR TENANT

MARRIED

You must consent in writing to any sale or giving up of the tenancy unless you have renounced your occupancy rights (see p 24). As long as you have not consented or renounced you are entitled to continue living there. Your consent may be dispensed with if the court, on an application by your husband or wife, is satisfied that you are withholding consent unreasonbly. You would be acting unreasonably for example if you did not want to continue living in the home and refused consent out of spite.

COHABITING

Your partner can give up the tenancy or sell the house without your consent. If you think this is likely you should apply to the court for an order giving you occupancy rights (see p 24), if you have not already got such an order. Once you have got occupancy rights you can ask the court to grant an interdict prohibiting your partner from selling or giving up the tenancy. Unless you act quickly the tenancy may have been given up or the home sold, and you will not be able to reverse matters.

Some local authorities do not require a sole tenant's husband or wife to consent to the tenant giving up the tenancy. If you find your husband or wife has given up the tenancy and you want to stay on in or return to the home, you should contact the housing department at once. Point out that you are legally entitled to continue living in the property.

YOU AND YOUR PARTNER ARE
JOINT OWNERS OR TENANTS

MARRIED

You must consent in writing to any sale or giving up of the tenancy. See p17 for the court's power to dispense with your consent. In the case of an owner-occupied home your husband or wife could alternatively apply to the court for an order requiring it to be sold. The court may however refuse to order a sale or postpone it — until the children no longer need it, for example.

COHABITING

Your partner can give up the tenancy for both without your consent. If this seems likely you should apply to the court for an interdict prohibiting your partner from doing this. Act quickly otherwise you will be too late. The home cannot be sold unless you and your partner join in the sale. The exception is where the court grants an order for sale. The court has no power to refuse or postpone this order if your partner applies for it.

YOUR PARTNER STOPS PAYING FOR THE HOME

TENANTS

If your partner stops paying the rent, the landlord will almost certainly take steps to bring the tenancy to an end. Once this has been done you have no further rights to remain in the home. In order to continue to live in the home you will therefore have to pay the rent legally due by your partner. You do not need your partner's permission to pay the rent, and the landlord is bound to accept rent offered by you.

As soon as you realise the rent is not being paid you should get in touch with the landlord and offer to pay the rent. See if they will agree to some arrangement for paying off the arrears by instalments. If legal proceedings for non-payment of rent have already been started, you are entitled to go along to the court in order to object as if you were the tenant. The court will not usually order eviction if you offer to pay off the arrears by reasonable instalments. You do not need your partner's permission to take these steps.

Where you and your partner are joint tenants each of you may be called on to pay the whole rent. Failure to pay the whole amount will mean that the landlord can take steps to bring the tenancy to an end and evict you.

You may be able to get help with the rent by way of Housing Benefit (see p 64). Benefit can be backdated for up to a year if you can show you were eligible during that period. This will help pay off arrears of rent. Another solution is to apply to the court for an order requiring your partner to reimburse you for the rent and arrears you paid on his or her behalf. You will probably not get the full amount back as you are getting the benefit of living in the home.

To prevent further trouble over non-payment of rent you could consider becoming the tenant in place of your partner or having the joint tenancy transferred to your name alone (see p 25).

OWNERS

If your partner stops paying the monthly repayments due to the building society, bank or other lender they will eventually call up the loan. This means the whole loan (not just the arrears) has to be repaid, otherwise they will evict you and sell the home. Your partner would be ill-advised to stop paying the instalments, since non-payers are blacklisted and may find it difficult to get credit in future. Also the home is unlikely to fetch as much in a forced sale as it would if sold normally.

Once you realise or suspect that payments are not being made you should contact the building society, bank or other lender as soon as possible if you want to continue living in the home, and explain the position to them. You are entitled to make the payments yourself and you do not need your partner's permission to do this. The lender may also require you to agree to pay off any arrears by instalments if they decide not to call up the loan.

Where you and your partner are joint borrowers each of you may be called on to pay the whole of the monthly instalments. Failure to pay the whole amount will result in the calling up of the loan and the sale of the home.

Help with the monthly payments may be obtained from Supplementary Benefit (see p 62). Another solution is to apply to the court for an order requiring your partner to reimburse you for the money you have paid the lender on his or her behalf. You will probably not get the full amount back from your partner as you are getting the benefit of living in the home.

SAFEGUARDING YOUR BELONGINGS

If your partner threatens to dispose of your belongings or refuses to hand them over to you, you can apply to the court. The court can grant an interdict prohibiting your partner from disposing of your belongings, or order your partner to hand over your belongings to you. If you are frightened to go in you could ask a friend to get them for you, or instruct a sheriff officer to collect them. In urgent cases an interdict will be granted as soon as you apply. What are your belongings and what are your partner's is often difficult to decide (see p 34 for further details).

If you are a (joint) owner or tenant you can use the home to store your belongings in, as long as this does not interfere with your partner's enjoyment of the property as a residence.

If you are not a (joint) tenant or owner, but have occupancy rights, you can bring reasonably required household goods into the home and your partner cannot insist that you remove them if you leave temporarily. You cannot use your partner's home as a storeroom for non-household goods, or for items you acquire after you leave, without your partner's permission.

PREVENTING YOUR PARTNER FROM REMOVING BASIC FURNITURE

If you have a right to occupy the home (as a sole or joint owner or tenant or a person with occupancy rights)you can secure the use of furniture and contents which belong to your partner. After all, it is not much use being entitled to live in the home if your partner can take everything away. You have to apply to the court for an order allowing you use and possession of various items. It may also be useful to apply for an interdict prohibiting your partner from removing any of these items without your agreement. The various items must be such as are reasonably necessary to enable you to use the home as a residence. For example, your partner would be able to remove books and a piano but not beds, tables or chairs.

SORTING OUT ACCOMMODATION

This chapter deals with your and your partner's legal rights concerning the home and suggests sources of alternative accommodation.

AM I ENTITLED TO STAY IN THE HOME?
FINDING OUT IF YOU ARE A (JOINT) TENANT OR OWNER
MARRIED TO THE TENANT OR OWNER
LIVING WITH THE TENANT OR OWNER
CAN THE TENANCY BE TRANSFERRED TO ME?
AM I LIABLE TO PAY THE RATES?
CAN I DO REPAIRS OR IMPROVEMENTS?
CAN I GET MY PARTNER OUT?
EXCLUSION ORDERS

STAYING PUT

WHERE CAN I FIND SOMEWHERE TO LIVE?
YOUR RIGHTS IF YOU ARE HOMELESS
YOUR NEW HOME AND YOUR PARTNER.

MOVING OUT

When you and your partner have decided to end your relationship and split up, one of the most important questions is where each of you is going to live. The choices are:—

- you leave while your partner remains in the home; OR
- your partner leaves while you remain in the home; OR
- both of you leave; OR
- both of you stay in the home.

The last option, both of you staying in the home, is unlikely to be a practical solution unless neither of you can find alternative accommodation or you are planning to move apart in the near future. Once a relationship is at an end it is often difficult for a couple to continue to live separate lives under the same roof.

You should try to agree with your partner who is to remain in the home. Do not rush - you may make a decision which you come to regret later. There is no easy way to decide what to do - each couple has to solve the problem in the light of their own circumstances. In the short term at any rate, it is usually best for the partner who is going to look after the children to remain in the home.

To help you come to a decision, the remainder of this chapter deals with the legal background to your and your partner's rights in the home. Of course legal issues are not the only ones to consider. Moving out is a great upheaval and may mean your losing contact with your friends and familiar surroundings. On the other hand, once you have got over the shock of splitting up, you may look on starting a new life elsewhere as a challenge, or an opportunity to move nearer to your own family. You may also want to move to a completely different part of the country to prevent your partner pestering or molesting you.

Finally, you and your partner cannot normally continue to live at the same standard as you did when you lived together. You should try to ensure that any drop in standards is shared, not borne by you alone.

STAYING PUT
AM I ENTITLED TO STAY IN THE HOME?

You are entitled to continue to occupy and live in the home which you and your partner lived in if:-

- you are the owner or tenant or a joint owner or joint tenant; OR
- you are married to your partner who is the owner or tenant; OR
- you are not married to your partner who is the owner or tenant, but the court has granted you occupancy rights (see p 24); OR
- you have some other legal right that entitles you to stay there – as a tenant of your partner for example.

Your partner may allow you to stay even if you have no legal entitlement, but this permission can be withdrawn at any time. You should be given reasonable notice to leave and your partner has no right to physically throw you and your belongings out on the street without obtaining an ejection order from the court.

If you have a right to live in the home, then you can have any of your children or your partner's children living with you. Your partner is not entitled to exclude the children (including those over 16) with the intention of forcing you to leave.

It is a criminal offence for your partner to harass you in order to get you to leave if you are entitled to stay.

Many of your rights depend on whether you are a tenant or owner. It is normally easy to find this out.

You are the sole tenant if only your name is on the lease or tenancy agreement, while you and your partner are joint tenants if both your names are there. You or your partner should have a copy of the lease or agreement; if not you should ask the landlord to let you see it. If you are not sure of your position — because for example, there is no written lease or agreement or the original document has been altered verbally later — you should seek advice from a Citizens Advice Bureau or a solicitor.

In the case of owner occupied property, whose name is on the document of title to the property is all important. You will never become the owner simply by paying the bills or making improvements. You are the sole owner if the title is in your name, while if you and your partner are both named you are joint owners. Joint ownership is very common nowadays amongst married and cohabiting couples. Unless the document of title says otherwise each joint owner has an equal share in the property.

If you want to find out about the title to your home you could ask your partner or the solicitor who was involved in the purchase. Another way is to ask at Register House in Edinburgh where a copy of the title to any property in Scotland may be inspected on payment of a fee.

In exceptional cases you can be declared to be the owner or joint owner even though you are not mentioned in the title. These are if:
- the person mentioned in the title has signed a written document agreeing that you are entitled to the home or a share of it; OR
- the person mentioned in the title swears in court that you are entitled to the home or a share of it; OR
- you prove that your name has been omitted from the title by mistake or fraud.

These are very uncommon situations.

FINDING OUT IF YOU ARE A (JOINT) TENANT OR OWNER

MARRIED TO THE TENANT OR OWNER

Where your husband or wife is the sole owner or tenant of the home you are entitled to continue to live in it or to return to live in it. But if your husband or wife won't let you in you will have to apply to the court for an order enforcing your rights (see p 12). These rights — called occupancy rights — normally last as long as you remain married, unless you renounce them (see below) or they have been suspended by a court order (see exclusion order on p 28). However, when you and your husband or wife get divorced the court dealing with the divorce can continue your occupancy rights.

Where your husband or wife is only a joint owner or tenant but you are not the other joint owner or tenant, you have occupancy rights in the home only if the other joint owner or tenant is not living in the house as well. For example if you and your wife live in a house owned jointly by your wife and her mother, you will have occupancy rights only as long as your mother-in-law is not living with you.

You can lose your occupancy rights by agreeing to renounce them — give them up. To be effective a renunciation must be in writing and signed in front of a notary public (most solicitors are notaries) and witnesses. Before you sign the notary must be satisfied that you are giving up your rights freely and not as the result of undue pressure. There are very few circumstances in which it will be in your interest to give up your rights. You are strongly advised never to renounce your rights without first seeking independent advice. While you are happily married occupancy rights may seem unimportant, but they can be extremely valuable on splitting up.

LIVING WITH THE TENANT OR OWNER

If your partner is the sole owner or tenant and you are not married to him or her, you have no right to continue to live in the home once you have been asked to leave. But you can apply to the court for an order granting you occupancy rights. You will need a solicitor to apply for the order on your behalf. If you have left the home you must apply promptly as a delay of more than a few weeks may prevent the court granting your application.

The court first decides whether you and your partner are cohabiting — living together as if you were husband and wife. You are likely to be regarded as cohabiting if you have lived together for more than a year and/or you and your partner have had children. The court goes on to consider whether you should be given the right to live in your partner's home. Important factors are your, your partner's and any children's need for accommodation and the possibility of your obtaining some other suitable place to live. If you are looking after young children you will very probably be allowed to stay on in the home.

The occupancy rights the court grants you last for 6 months initially. You can however apply for further extensions, which last for 6 months at a time. But the court is most unlikely to allow you to stay on indefinitely by repeatedly renewing your occupancy rights, especially if your partner owns the home.

On splitting up you may want the tenancy of the home to be in your name, instead of your partner's or jointly with your partner. This can be done by applying to the landlord or the court.

As long as your partner and the landlord agree, the tenancy can be made over to you. Although you are not legally responsible for any arrears of rent due by your partner, in practice the landlord may try to "persuade" you to pay them. See a solicitor if this happens.

Where the home is rented from a public sector landlord (district/islands council, SSHA, New Town Development Corporation, housing association etc.) and your partner refuses to transfer you can ask the landlord to apply to the court for an order terminating your partner's tenancy. Partner includes ex-husband or wife. The court will grant this order if satisfied that other suitable accommodation is available for your partner and that the home is to be relet to you because you and your partner don't want to live together. Unless you are divorced you can also use the procedure discribed below. You have to use that procedure if the landlord is not a public sector landlord or won't agree to apply.

Where your partner and/or the landlord refuse to agree to the transfer you can apply to the court for a tenancy transfer order, either separately or as part of your separation or divorce proceedings. To apply you have to be married to the tenant or be a cohabiting partner with occupancy rights (see p24). But you can apply for occupancy rights at the same time as you apply for a tenancy transfer order. In deciding whether or not to grant a tenancy transfer order, the court looks at all the circumstances. Attention is paid to both your and your partner's

CAN THE TENANCY BE TRANSFERRED TO ME?

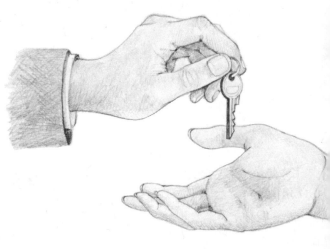

needs for accommodation and ability to find other accommodation. Where there are children their needs are usually the deciding factor. If you need the home for the children in your custody the court will almost certainly give you the tenancy. The landlord is entitled to object to your application. While the court will listen to arguments about your inability to pay the rent or be a good tenant, it may overrule them. You should be prepared to satisfy the court that the landlord's fears are groundless or exaggerated. You can get help with the rent by Housing Benefit (see p64).

Once you become the tenant in place of your partner you are then liable to pay the rent and carry out the other conditions of the lease — keeping the garden tidy for example. But you are not liable for any arrears of rent due by your partner. As the new tenant you can require your ex-husband/wife or cohabiting partner to leave the home, but to get your husband or wife out legally an exclusion order (see p.28) is necessary.

Your partner's share of a joint tenancy with you can be transferred so that you become the sole tenant. This can be done by agreement or by application to the court as above.

AM I LIABLE TO PAY THE RATES?

If you and your husband are entered in the assessment roll as occupiers, either of you can be called on to pay the full amount, however the property is owned and occupied. On leaving you should contact your Regional Assessor to have your name deleted.

Where only your partner is on the assessment roll he or she is normally liable for the rates. But you will have to pay if your partner leaves you in the home and doesn't pay. Housing Benefit (see p.64) is available to help pay the rates.

CAN I DO REPAIRS OR IMPROVEMENTS?

Your rights depend on whether the home is owned or rented and what sort of right you have to live in it (see below). Bear in mind that improvements involving structural alterations (such as building a garage or knocking two rooms into one) will usually require building control permission and may need planning permission as well. Check with your district council before you start.

Where the home is rented you may need the landlord's permission to do maintenance, repairs or improvements, or the landlord may be responsible for keeping the property in repair. Check the lease or tenancy agreement or ask the landlord before you start. If the home is rented from the district council and they are obliged to carry out repairs, you may be able to get modest repairs done yourself and ask them to reimburse you, rather than wait for them to do the work.

You do not need your partner's agreement to do any repairs etc. You can apply to the court for an order requiring your husband or wife (if living in the home) to contribute to the cost of essential repairs (mending a leaking roof or replacing dangerous wiring for example) or repairs he or she has agreed to. If you and your partner are not married you can apply only if he or she has been granted occupancy rights.

YOU ARE THE SOLE OWNER/TENANT

You do not need your partner's agreement for essential repairs. If you want to carry out other work and your partner won't agree you can apply to the court for authorisation. Unless the court orders otherwise the cost of any work including essential repairs is shared equally.

YOU AND YOUR PARTNER ARE JOINT OWNERS/TENANTS

You do not need your partner's agreement for essential repairs. You can apply to the court for an order requiring your partner to contribute to the cost. If you want to do non-essential repairs or improvements and your partner won't agree you can apply to the court for authorisation. You will have to pay the whole cost yourself.

YOU HAVE OCCUPANCY RIGHTS AS THE PARTNER OF THE OWNER OR TENANT

You are not entitled to do any repairs etc without your partner's agreement. If you do you are liable for the whole cost yourself, and you may be required to restore the property to its previous state.

YOU HAVE NO OCCUPANCY RIGHTS

Being entitled to stay put in the home is only half of the battle, since you will normally want it to yourself. This means your partner has to move out. If it will not provoke violence you could try persuading him or her to go voluntarily before you take any of these steps below. If your partner will not go voluntarily you can :

CAN I GET MY PARTNER OUT?

> SHUT HIM OR HER OUT. You will in most cases be committing a criminal offence by doing this and your partner may take legal proceedings against you (see p 11). The exceptional case is where you are the sole owner or tenant AND you and your partner are not married to

each other AND your partner has not been granted occupancy rights by the court. Here your partner is obliged to leave once you have told him or her to go. You should however give a reasonable period of notice and you are not entitled to throw your partner and your partner's belongings out into the street without getting an ejection order from the court.

GO TO COURT FOR AN EXCLUSION ORDER. If you get it your partner will no longer be entitled to live in or be in the home even if he or she is a (joint) owner or tenant.

EXCLUSION ORDERS

To obtain an exclusion order you will need to demonstrate to the court that it is necessary to protect you or your children from any conduct (or threatened or reasonably apprehended conduct) by your partner that injures or could injure your physical or mental health or that of your children. Even where you satisfy this test, the court still looks at all the circumstances of the case — such as your and your partner's conduct and finances and the needs of any children — to make sure that exclusion would be reasonable. A most important factor is the need of the children for suitable accommodation. If you were forced to leave home because of domestic violence and have to live with the children in cramped, temporary accommodation, the court is likely to order your partner out.

You can apply for an exclusion order while you are still in the home or after you have been forced to leave. Your application for an exclusion order is almost certain to be opposed by your partner, so that your solicitor will need all the supporting evidence that can be obtained. This might include statements from neighbours, police reports of previous incidents, certificates from your doctor as to injuries to your health, and the unsuitable nature of your temporary accommodation if you have moved out. If you can foresee your need for an exclusion order you should try to tell your neighbours and your doctor about your injuries as they occur, and what they were caused by, so that they will be in a position to give evidence later.

Where you and your partner are cohabitees and your partner is the sole owner or tenant you must have occupancy rights (see p24) before the court will consider your application for an exclusion order. But you can apply for occupancy rights and an exclusion order at the same time.

An exclusion order normally lasts until it is cancelled by the court or until divorce (married couples only). However, the divorce court can continue the exclusion order after divorce, but it will only do so if it decides to award you the right after divorce to occupy your ex-husband's or wife's home. If you are a cohabitee and the home is not in your name the court is unlikely to exclude your partner for more than a few months – long enough to enable you to find alternative accommodation or to apply for the tenancy to be transferred to you.

MOVING OUT
WHERE CAN I FIND SOMEWHERE TO LIVE?

If you decide to leave home you will have to find somewhere else to live. See p 13 for emergency accommodation.
The main sources of permanent housing are:—
- local authority
- housing associations
- private landlords
- buying your own home
- shared ownership housing
- mobile homes.

LOCAL AUTHORITY

In most areas council houses are in short supply and there will be a waiting list. In particular there is very little accommodation available for single people. Ask your district or islands council how it gives different people priority for housing. If you count as a person in "priority need" your council may be bound to provide you with permanent accommodation under the Housing (Homeless Persons) Act — see p 31.

HOUSING ASSOCIATIONS

There are a number of national and local housing associations that provide rented accommodation. The "yellow pages" will give details of associations in your area.
Alternatively contact:
Scottish Federation of Housing Associations,
42 York Place,
Edinburgh.

PRIVATE RENTED HOUSING

Accommodation and estate agencies or solicitors are the best sources; newspapers and newsagents also advertise property to let. Private rented accommodation tends to be expensive but you could consider taking it and then applying for a "fair rent" to be fixed. But check you have some security of tenure before you do this, and that fair rents for similar houses in the area are less than your rent (contact your local Rent Registration Service office — address in the telephone book).

Housing Benefit (see p 64) is available to help pay the rent; you can claim it even though the rent is above a fair rent. Single Payments (see p 64) may be obtainable from the DHSS to meet returnable deposits, rent in advance, or the cost of basic furniture if you can only find unfurnished accommodation and you have no furniture of your own.

You should also consider what security of tenure you will have. This is a very complex subject. If you are in doubt you should seek advice from a Citizens Advice Bureau or a solicitor.

OWNER-OCCUPIED HOUSING

Buying a house is expensive although it may be better than renting in the long run if you can afford it. You will need some cash even if you can get a loan for most of the price. If you and your partner own your home you may be able to put your share towards a new home for yourself. The amount of loan you can get depends on your income and the value placed on the home you are thinking of buying by the lender's surveyor. You should consult a solicitor before you start looking around, and certainly before you sign any offer to buy, because you may otherwise commit yourself to something you cannot fulfill.

If you have difficulty in obtaining a loan from a building society or bank ask your district or islands council to nominate you under the Building Societies Support Lending Scheme.

SHARED OWNERSHIP HOUSING

This is a mixture of ownership and tenancy. Shared ownership schemes are not common but may be worth looking for. The amount of loan required is smaller than if you bought the home completely. Contact the Housing Corporation, Roseberry House, Haymarket Terrace, Edinburgh for further details.

MOBILE HOMES

There are not many sites with caravans that can be occupied all the year round. Most of them tend to be situated away from shops, schools and workplaces. The owner – occupier of a residential caravan is entitled to an agreement with the site-owner which gives security of tenure for at least 5 years. A caravan is a depreciating asset so you are unlikely to get back what you paid for it. Housing Benefit is available to help with the caravan and site rent if you rent it.

YOUR RIGHTS IF YOU ARE HOMELESS

If you are:—
- homeless or threatened with homelessness; AND
- in priority need; AND
- not intentionally homeless; AND
- have a local connection;

your local housing authority is obliged to provide you with (or see that you are provided with) suitable permanent accommodation. The type of permanent accommodation you will be offered varies from authority to authority and the way in which authorities interpret their duties varies also. If you are dissatisfied with their decision you can apply to the Court of Session for it to be reviewed.

You are homeless if you have no accommodation or you are unable to use your accommodation because you have been thrown out, or you would run the risk of violence if you lived there. You still count as homeless even if you are staying in a refuge or other emergency accommodation because of the violence at home. On the other hand you will not be regarded as homeless simply because you and your partner have decided to split up and find alternative accommodation.

The term "threatened with homelessness" means that it is likely that you will be homeless within the next 28 days — for example if you are a tenant about to be evicted or have been told by your partner with whom you are cohabiting to leave.

To be in priority need you must :
- have dependent children (which need not be your own, nor is it necessary that the court has awarded you custody of them); OR
- be pregnant; OR
- have lost your accommodation due to an emergency (such as a fire); OR
- you or a member of your household are vulnerable as a result of old age, handicap or other special reason. The Code of Guidance on the Act prepared by the Scottish Development Department suggests that women without children who have suffered domestic violence should be regarded as vulnerable.

If the local authority considers that you are intentionally homeless (you deliberately didn't pay the rent for example) then they need only offer you temporary accommodation. The Code suggests that victims of domestic

violence who have fled their homes should not be treated as intentionally homeless. But the local authority may not agree. They may adopt the attitude that victims should stay in the home and apply to the court to have their violent partners excluded or prohibited from treating them violently by interdict. If you faced with this argument you should point out that exclusion orders are difficult to get and that interdicts do not necessarily protect you from your partner's violent behaviour.

Normally your application for accommodation would be made to the authority which you have a local connection with (living or working in their area for example). But you can apply for permanent accommodation to another local authority in Scotland, England and Wales in order to escape from your violent partner. As long as you can show that you would be in danger from violence if you stayed in your own area, you need not have a connection with the authority to which you apply under the Act.

YOUR NEW HOME AND YOUR PARTNER

When you do find new accommodation for yourself, your former partner has no rights to live in it or to be in it without your consent. This is because it is not a matrimonial home — a home for you and your partner; it is a home you got for yourself (and any children). If your partner attempts to get in, or refuses to leave after you have told him or her to go, you can call the police. You may find the police will deal more sympathetically with your case than if you were still living with your partner, as it is no longer a "domestic dispute".

Another way of dealing with your partner molesting you or causing trouble is to apply to the court for an interdict. This interdict may be enforced in the same way as other interdicts (see p 10) but if you are divorced from your partner or were not married to him or her, you cannot have a power of arrest attached to your interdict.

UNTANGLING YOUR FINANCES AND PROPERTY

This chapter provides guidance for married and cohabiting couples on how to sort out their property and financial affairs.

COHABITING COUPLES
MARRIED COUPLES

WHO OWNS THE HOUSEHOLD GOODS?

DISAGREEMENTS ABOUT THE BELONGINGS

USING YOUR PARTNER'S FURNITURE

YOU AND/OR YOUR PARTNER OWN THE HOME
YOU AND/OR YOUR PARTNER RENT THE HOME

WHAT ABOUT THE HOME?

WHO OWNS THE SAVINGS AND INVESTMENTS?

AM I LIABLE FOR MY PARTNER'S DEBTS?

HIRE PURCHASE GOODS

FUEL BILLS

WHO TO INFORM ABOUT SPLITTING UP

OTHER TASKS TO CONSIDER

While you and your partner lived together you will have rented or bought a home and bought furnishings and appliances for it. You will also have bought things yourselves and for each other. You may have opened joint accounts with a bank or building society or undertaken joint financial commitments such as a building society loan or a hire purchase agreement. On splitting up you will have to work out with your partner what to do about the home, the belongings, savings and financial commitments.

You and your partner should try to agree on these matters if possible. Going to court can be expensive and the legal expenses may easily exceed the value of the items under dispute. Even if you win you may not recover all your expenses from your partner. To help you and your partner to reach a mutually acceptable solution this chapter sets out the legal rules relating to ownership of property and liability for debts.

WHO OWNS THE HOUSEHOLD GOODS?

Deciding who owns the household goods and similar articles is often very difficult. This is because it may be necessary to think back many years to when the item was bought to find out who bought it and what their intentions were then.
There will be different rules for married and cohabiting couples when section 25 of the Family Law (Scotland) Act 1985 is brought into force. Until then the rules for cohabiting couples apply to married couples as well.

COHABITING COUPLES

As a general rule you are the owner of articles which:—
- you acquired before you lived together or after you split up, OR
- you bought, OR
- you were given.

There is no assumption of joint ownership of household goods or any other items. Your goods continue to belong to you even though they are situated in your partner's home or you and your partner both use them, unless you have actually given them to your partner or made it clear that they are to be joint property.

Normally you own any article which you buy while living with your partner even if you used your partner's money or joint money instead of your own. This rule does not apply if you bought things on behalf of your partner — for example if she asked you to buy a typewriter for her. In this case the article belongs to your partner. Using your partner's money when you have no right to do so could be theft or embezzlement and you could be prosecuted as well as being made to repay the money.

If someone makes you a gift of an article then it will belong to you. This simple rule can often be difficult to apply because in the case of "gifts" from one partner to the other the giver may not have made his or her intention clear. Unless your partner actually made it clear, or it is clear from the nature of the article (such as clothes or jewellery which only you can wear) that a gift was intended, it will be assumed that the article was merely lent to you or that you were simply allowed to use it.

Another difficulty is that where other people give a present it may have been intended for both you and your partner or for only one of you. Who owns it depends on the intention of the giver. Sometimes this is clear from what was said or written at the time of the gift — wedding presents are normally addressed to both bride and groom. Where the giver's intention was not expressed, you have to try and work it out from the nature of the present and the circumstances in which it was given. A birthday present, for instance, is obviously intended for the person whose birthday it is.

MARRIED COUPLES

It is assumed that the household goods belong to the husband and wife equally. Joint ownership is only an assumption; you may still be able to establish that you are the sole owner of a particular item, but the mere fact that you bought it does not help your claim. Household goods means furniture, furnishings and articles such as beds, tables, chairs, carpets, curtains, wardrobes, chests; but also includes pictures, books, refrigerators, televisions, pianos and washing machines. On the other hand money, cars and pets are not counted as household goods.

For joint ownership to be assumed the household goods must have been bought for your and your husband's or wife's "joint domestic purposes" — for furnishing the home, for joint use in the home or for child care. But if you have golf clubs or a micro-computer for yourself or equipment for your business, these would not have been bought for a joint domestic purpose so that the rule that the person who bought them is normally the owner would apply, (see p 34).

Articles which you owned before marriage are not assumed to be joint property. They will continue to belong to you even though they are situated in your husband's or wife's home and both of you use them, unless you have actually given them to your husband or wife or made it clear that they are to be joint property. The assumption of joint ownership also does not apply to items you acquired after you split up.

The rules relating to gifts are the same as for cohabiting couples (see p 34).

DISAGREEMENTS ABOUT THE BELONGINGS

If you and your partner cannot agree who owns what, or how the belongings are to be divided, you may have to go to court to resolve the dispute. However, the legal expenses may be more than the items are worth, and even if you win you may find yourself out of pocket.

Where your ownership of an article is admitted or proved the court can:—
- order your partner to return the article to you or its value if he or she no longer has it; AND
- authorise sheriff officers to search for the article and hand it over to you; AND
- interdict (prohibit) your partner from removing or threatening to remove the article from your possession in the future.

If you and your partner are joint owners of an article and you cannot agree what is to happen to it, you can apply to the court for an order requiring the article to be sold and the money divided between you.

The court on granting a divorce has power to order transfers of property. In this way you could become sole owner of items you and your husband or wife own jointly or become the owner of items belonging solely to your husband or wife. Obviously you can only apply to the court if you are married and have grounds for divorce proceedings (see Chapter 8). Another solution is to apply for a use and possession order (see below). This is not tied to divorce proceedings and is available if you are married or cohabiting.

USING YOUR PARTNER'S FURNITURE

You can apply to the court for an order (a "use and possession order") allowing you to use in the home your partner's furniture and furnishings which are situated there. You may also wish to apply for an interdict preventing your partner from removing the items you have been given the use of. To qualify you must be entitled to occupy the home either as a (joint) tenant or owner or as a person with occupancy rights. A use and possession order could be very useful if you want to go on living in the home, but all the furniture is your partner's and he or she intends to remove it. An empty house would not be much good to you if you had no means of refurnishing it.

The court can only give you use and possession of items which are reasonably necessary to enable the home to be used as a residence. Things like beds, tables, chairs, cookers, fires, china, cutlery, carpets and curtains sufficient for your (and any children's) needs would be included, but cars are definitely excluded. Whether you would be given the use of items such as a piano, television or a washing machine would depend on your circumstances. For example if you were looking after very young children a washing machine might be regarded as reasonably necessary.

WHAT ABOUT THE HOME?

YOU AND/OR YOUR PARTNER RENT THE HOME

If neither you nor your partner want to continue to live in the home, it is best to give up the tenancy. This is done by giving notice to the landlord. The period of notice depends on the terms of the lease or tenancy agreement. The landlord may be willing to accept shorter notice; on the other hand, particularly in the case of a fixed-term tenancy, the landlord may not be prepared to accept termination before the due date.

If you want to stay on and your partner agrees to this, you could have the tenancy transferred to you (see p 25 for how to do this). You should consider carefully whether you can afford to pay the rent and other running costs, since once you become the tenant you will be liable for these. For assistance with paying the rent see Housing Benefit (p 64); for fixing a fair rent see p 29.

Your partner may not agree to your staying on in the home. Your rights to do so and to exclude your partner are dealt with in Chapters 2 and 3. See Chapter 2 also for ways of preventing your partner from bringing the tenancy to an end without your agreement.

YOU AND/OR YOUR PARTNER
OWN THE HOME

SELLING — If neither you nor your partner want to carry on living in the home after splitting up, it is best to sell it and use the money to get separate accommodation for each of you.

The money from the sale of the home belongs to the owner or to the joint owners (see p 23 for how to find out if you are an owner or joint owner). If you are not the owner or a joint owner, and your partner is not prepared to pay part of the proceeds to you when the home is sold you can:

start divorce proceedings claiming a lump sum or a transfer of the home to you and meanwhile asking the court to make an order prohibiting or preventing a sale or "freezing" the money from a sale.	This applies if you are married to the sole owner and you have grounds for divorce (see Chapter 8).
apply to the court for an order requiring your partner to repay to you the money you contributed when the home was bought.	This applies if you are married or cohabiting with the sole owner and your contribution was made not more than 5 years from the date of your application. If you are cohabiting you must have occupancy rights or be granted them at the same time (see p 24).

Other methods include:

refusing to consent to the sale	This applies if you have occupancy rights as the husband or wife of the sole owner. Your refusal to consent may however be overruled by the court (see p 17).
applying to the court for occupancy rights and an interdict prohibiting the sale.	This applies if you are cohabiting with the sole owner

These methods will not by themselves give you a share of the money. But taking or threatening to take such action may lead to your partner "buying you off." It would be wise to get any agreement about the sharing of money resulting from the sale of the home prepared by a solicitor, so that it can be enforced easily if the need arises.

If you want to stay on in the home and your partner is agreeable to this, you may want to become the owner. You should think carefully and seek advice from a solicitor before agreeing to buy the home (or your partner's share in it) from your partner. The building society, bank or other lender will also have to be consulted and agree to the transfer unless their loan is to be paid off. On the other hand you may be content to leave the ownership as it is and simply continue to occupy the home. From your partner's point of view this has the disadvantage of tying up in the home money which he or she may need to buy other accommodation. Another possibility is for you to forgo your financial claims against your partner in exchange for your partner's (share of the) home. This applies mainly to married couples. Both of you should get legal advice before agreeing to this.

STAYING ON

Where you and your partner own the home jointly both of you have to agree to a sale and the money from the sale is shared between you. If you and your partner can't agree about whether the home should be sold, an application for sale can be made to the court. In the case of a married couple the court may refuse to order a sale or postpone it. But where the owners are not married a sale will always be ordered.

Where you are living in your partner's home or a jointly owned home you should agree with your partner who is going to pay the running costs (see Chapter 6 for ways of saving tax). If you can't agree the court can apportion the costs as it thinks fit.

Your partner may not agree to your staying on in the home, perhaps because he or she wants to live there or sell it. See Chapters 2 and 3 for your rights to live there and to exclude your partner. Ways of preventing your partner from selling the home without your agreement are dealt with in Chapter 2. Another method of being able to stay in the home, which is available if you are married and have grounds for divorce (see Chapter 8), is to start divorce proceedings and claim either to have the home made over to you on divorce or to have the right to occupy it after divorce. The court may, however, take the view that it would be better for the home to be sold.

WHO OWNS THE SAVINGS AND INVESTMENTS?

The fact that a bank, building society or similar account is in your name does not necessarily mean you own the money in it; it just means you can withdraw it. Ownership depends on where the money came from and what the intention was in putting it into your account. For example, if only you put your pay or savings in then the money belongs entirely to you. On the other hand, if your partner has put money into your account so that you can pay your partner's business expenses whilst he or she is abroad, then the money belongs to your partner.

The ownership of money in a joint account in names of you and your partner depends on how much each of you contributed and your intentions in opening the joint account. If only you put money in, but you made the account joint so that your partner could sign cheques or withdraw money as well, the money will belong entirely to you. On the other hand if your intention was to pool resources with your partner (which is more likely nowadays), or if both you and your partner put money in, you are both joint owners.

Investments, such as stocks and shares, belong to you if they are in your name. If the certificate is in the name of you and your partner, each of you own an equal half share wherever the money came from.

If you and your partner cannot agree on how to deal with the money (savings and investments) you will have to go to court. This is generally worth doing only if there is a sizeable sum at stake. On divorce the court can divide up the money by ordering one of you to pay a lump sum to the other. The factors that it takes into account in deciding how much (if any) to award are discussed in Chapter 5.

AM I LIABLE FOR MY PARTNER'S DEBTS?

The general rule is that you are not liable for your partner's debts, hire purchase or other financial commitments. But you can be made to pay if:—

- you agreed to act as guarantor. This means that if your partner whose debts you have guaranteed fails to pay, you will be required to pay instead. It is then up to you to try to get the amount you paid back from your partner.

- you have agreed to be "jointly and severally liable" with your partner. Common examples of joint and several liability are rent due by joint tenants, repayments due on a joint loan, and an overdraft on a joint account. You can be called on to pay the whole amount. If you do you are entitled to ask your partner to reimburse you for the half share you have paid on his or her behalf.

● your husband, wife or child (but not cohabiting partner) died without leaving enough to pay for the funeral and the local authority carried out the funeral. They are entitled to recover the cost from you.

● you are living in the matrimonial home and the court has ordered you to pay the building society (or bank) loan instalments due by your absent spouse. This rule applies only to husbands and wives.

● you authorised your partner to buy something on your behalf. As long as it was made clear to the supplier that your partner was only ordering on your behalf, your partner is not liable even if you don't pay. You can also be liable if you have in the past paid for goods ordered by your partner, although you did not expressly authorise the present purchase.

If you are a mail order catalogue agent you are not liable for goods supplied to a customer who fails to pay even if the customer is your partner. Neither are you liable for purchases made by your partner with his or her own credit card unless the bank or other account they are charged against is a joint account or one that you have guaranteed.

HIRE PURCHASE GOODS

You are only liable to pay for an article on hire purchase or conditional sale agreement if you signed the form as the purchaser (or a joint purchaser) or as guarantor (see p 40). Otherwise if your partner fails to keep up the payments for his or her purchases the hire purchase company must sue your partner not you. They are also entitled to repossess the goods but need a court order if more than one-third of the price due has been paid. Until they are repossessed you can carry on using the goods with the agreement of your partner.

If you want to keep the goods you can contact the hire purchase company and get the agreement transferred to your name. When paid for the goods will belong to you, but you become liable to make the payments under the agreement in future and may be sued if you fail to do so. Alternatively, you can simply pay each instalment as it falls due instead of your partner. In this way you will continue to have the use of the goods and not commit yourself to making future payments. But the drawback is when the goods are fully paid for, they will belong to your partner not you.

FUEL BILLS

Electricity and gas bills are payable by the person who signed the agreement for supply. This is the person to whom the bills are addressed. The fuel board is entitled to disconnect the supply (a charge is made for reconnection) if a bill is not paid, and legal proceedings will be taken against the person to recover the amount due. You should contact the board at once if you find yourself in difficulties.

If the person who signed the agreement has left ask for the meter to be read and a new supply agreement to be prepared in your name.

If the board are satisfied that your partner has genuinely left you (a letter from your solicitor may help) they will pursue your partner for the unpaid bills rather than disconnect you. You may be able to recover part at least of the money you spent in paying your partner's bills by applying to the court for an order apportioning the bills.

WHO TO INFORM ABOUT SPLITTING UP

BANK

You should contact your branch if you want to open, close or change the names on an account. It is probably better to close a joint account on splitting up because then your partner will not be able to withdraw money that you put in, and you will not be liable for any overdraft that your partner incurs afterwards.

INLAND REVENUE

If you and your partner are married to each other, you should inform your tax office of any separation since this alters the way in which you will be taxed in the future. See Chapter 6 for further details.

LANDLORD

When you and your partner have decided to split up you should contact the landlord either to make arrangements for giving up the tenancy or to see if the partner of the tenant can take over the tenancy. Don't be frightened of contacting the landlord. As long as you are married to the tenant or are a cohabiting partner with occupancy rights the landlord cannot put you out simply because the tenant no longer lives there. You can of course still be ejected (a court order is necessary) if the rent is not paid (see p 18).

You should contact the building society, bank or other lender if you and your partner plan to alter the ownership of the home between yourselves. In theory building societies can refuse to agree as long as the loan remains outstanding, but in practice they will agree to an alteration, provided they are satisfied the loan instalments will continue to be paid. If you, as new owner, do not have sufficient income, your partner or another person may be asked to act as guarantor. You will need a solicitor to prepare the necessary documents altering the ownership.

See p 19 for what to do if your partner stops paying the loan instalments.

BUILDING SOCIETY

You should inform your local DHSS office of your splitting up if you are receiving any state benefit. The separation will probably affect the rate of benefit or even whether you are still entitled to it. You should tell them promptly because if you are overpaid as a result of not telling them, you will be liable to pay back the extra and may be prosecuted for receiving benefit which you were not entitled to. On the other hand you may become eligible for benefits. See p 4 for how to obtain confidential advice.

DHSS

Where you are jointly liable with your partner for goods bought with a credit card you should think about contacting the credit organisation to see if this agreement can be ended. Otherwise you may be held liable for goods your partner buys after you have split up. See p 41 for what to do about hire purchase goods.

CREDIT COMPANIES

If the agreement for the supply of electricity, gas or the telephone is in your name you should contact the fuel board or British Telecom on moving out. Otherwise you may find yourself having to pay for future supplies used by your partner.

FUEL BOARDS AND BRITISH TELECOM

OTHER TASKS TO CONSIDER

WILLS

On splitting up you and your partner should consider making wills or altering your wills.

If you do not leave a will your husband or wife may inherit most of your estate as long as you have not been divorced. On the other hand you may wish to leave something to your former partner whom you were living with but not married to. Unless you make a will he or she will inherit nothing.

You should consider altering your will on splitting up. If you do not cancel bequests to your former partner he or she may still be entitled to them even after divorce. You should see a solicitor about making a new will, but remember that you can't completely disinherit your husband or wife, because as long as you are still married he or she can claim legal rights (see p 58).

NOMINATIONS

Several organisations, such as friendly societies, allow you to nominate a person to whom the amount in your account or benefits are to paid on your death. If you have nominated your partner you should, on splitting up, consider whether to cancel the nomination. If you decide to cancel it, you will need to contact the organisation and fill in the appropriate forms.

LIFE INSURANCE

Many people have life insurance policies on their own lives in which the benefits are payable to their executors or their partners. In the latter case you should think about whether the policy ought to be changed when you and your partner split up. You should not surrender the policy or stop paying the premiums without first consulting a solicitor or accountant. It may be possible to alter the terms of the policy by agreement. The court on granting a divorce can alter the terms of a life policy taken out under the Married Women's Policies of Assurance Acts as part of the financial settlement.

Similar problems arise when one partner insures the other's life, or when a joint policy is taken out on both lives.

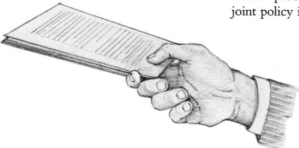

FUTURE FINANCES — MONEY FROM YOUR PARTNER

This chapter deals mainly with maintenance from your partner for yourself and any children, and financial arrangements on divorce. A final section contains information on your rights to inherit from your former partner.

WHO CAN I GET MAINTENANCE FROM? *HOW TO GET MAINTENANCE* *HOW MUCH MAINTENANCE WILL I GET?*	*SEPARATION*
WHAT CAN I APPLY FOR? *HOW THE COURT DECIDES WHAT TO DO* *THE COURT'S ORDERS*	*DIVORCE*
CAN THE AMOUNT BE CHANGED? *WHAT HAPPENS IF MY PARTNER DIES?* *WHAT HAPPENS IF I REMARRY OR COHABIT?* *WHAT HAPPENS IF MY PARTNER IS MADE BANKRUPT?* *ENFORCING YOUR MAINTENANCE*	*CHANGES IN MAINTENANCE*
WHERE A WILL IS LEFT *WHERE NO WILL IS LEFT* *SURVIVORSHIP| DESTINATIONS* *YOUR RIGHTS UNDER YOUR* *PARTNER'S PENSION SCHEME*	*YOUR INHERITANCE RIGHTS*

The type of financial support you can get from your partner for yourself and the children varies with the stage you have reached in splitting up. On separation you can claim aliment from your husband or wife but not from your cohabiting partner. The children can claim aliment from their parents whether or not they were married to each other. Aliment is the Scottish legal term for maintenance payable by parents to their children, by husbands to their wives and by wives to their husbands. On divorce you can claim from your ex-husband or ex-wife a lump sum, a transfer of property, or a periodical allowance (maintenance) for yourself, as well as aliment for any children.

As it usually the woman who is seeking financial support from her partner, this chapter is written on that basis for the sake of simplicity. However the points apply equally to men seeking support from their wives unless stated otherwise.

SEPARATION
WHO CAN I GET MAINTENANCE FROM?

Your husband has a legal obligation to aliment (or provide for) you as long as you remain married to him. If you are not married to your partner he has no legal obligation to aliment you although he may agree to do so.

Your husband or cohabiting partner has a legal obligation to aliment his own children (including adopted children) and any child he has accepted as a child of his family (such as a child of yours by a previous marriage). A child who is being fostered is not counted as being accepted as a child of the family.

The liability to aliment a child lasts until the child is 18, or if the child is at university, college or another further education establishment or is being trained for employment, a trade or a profession, until 25. Once a child reaches 25 liability ceases, even if the child is not earning a living.

HOW TO GET MAINTENANCE

While you and your husband or partner and any children live together as a family aliment is given by provision of a home, food, clothing and other things suitable to your standard of living.

On separation aliment is usually given entirely in money (so much a week or month). Your husband or partner could aliment you by providing a home and paying the bills for it, but this suffers from a tax disadvantage (see p 74). You can get aliment for yourself and any children by payments made:

- voluntarily; OR
- under an enforceable written agreement (an agreement that contains a legally binding obligation to pay aliment), sometimes called a separation agreement; OR
- under a court order.

The advantages and disadvantages of each method are shown in the accompanying chart. Tax questions are discussed in Chapter 6.

VOLUNTARY PAYMENTS

ADVANTAGES
Does not count as payee's taxable income. Amount payable easily altered. No legal fees.

DISADVANTAGES
Not legally enforceable. No tax allowance given to payer. Have to go to court if can't agree how much should be paid.

ENFORCEABLE AGREEMENT

ADVANTAGES
Legally enforceable. Agreement may provide for alteration if circumstances change. Tax allowance given to payer (but where child's aliment is concerned only if agreement is registered: see p 71).

DISADVANTAGES
Counts as taxable income of payee. Legal fees payable but legal aid may be available. Tax is deducted from every payment (even a "small maintenance payment") by payer. Payee may be able to reclaim it.

COURT ORDER

ADVANTAGES
Legally enforceable. Tax allowance given to payer. Can be paid without deduction of tax if "small maintenance payment" (see p 70).

DISADVANTAGES
Alterable only by another court order. Legal fees payable but legal aid may be available. Counts as taxable income of payee. Only available if legally entitled to ailment. Slower than other methods and may involve publicity.

You as the parent or the person having custody or care of a child can claim aliment on his or her behalf. Once children reach 18 they have to bring legal proceedings for themselves.

You cannot get aliment for yourself from your cohabiting partner by means of a court order because he has no legal obligation to aliment you. He may agree to provide for you voluntarily or sign an enforceable agreement. But he does have a legal obligation to aliment his own children or children he has accepted as children of his family (see p 46).

HOW MUCH MAINTENANCE WILL I GET?

The amount of aliment payable voluntarily or under an enforceable agreement depends on what was arranged between the parties concerned.

In legal proceedings for aliment the court will only award what is reasonable. It is not possible to give any rule of thumb since what is considered reasonable depends very much on the individual circumstances of each case and the views of the judge hearing it. The main factors taken into account are:-

- the applicant's needs and resources; AND
- the payer's needs and resources; AND
- the standard of living previously enjoyed by the applicant AND
- the length of your marriage (this affects your aliment not the children's).

Your husband can defend your claim for aliment on the ground that he is willing to have you living with him and provide for you in that way. The court will then look at all the circumstances to see whether his offer is reasonable. If the court thinks it is reasonable your claim will be dismissed. It would be unreasonable for you to have to accept your husband's offer if he had committed adultery, behaved violently or unreasonably, or his home was not suitable.

Your needs depend on some extent on the standard of living enjoyed when living together. You cannot normally expect to maintain this standard, but you should not be reduced to the "bread line" if you lived well before and your husband can afford to pay a decent aliment.

Needs are primarily your own needs, but the court MAY take into account the fact that you support other dependants (such as an aged parent or a cohabiting partner) even though you have no legal obligation to do so. Where you have a legal obligation to support (a new child for example) this MUST be taken into account in assessing needs. Your husband's needs are assessed in the same way. Your and your husband's resources generally means income. Each of you will have to give evidence of income in the shape of recent pay-slips, income tax returns etc. Both of you can be ordered to provide evidence of your resources. If you are living with another man the court will usually take that into account and refuse to award you aliment for yourself but he cannot be ordered to disclose his resources.

Where a child is claiming aliment the court will take into account any contribution to the child's aliment which is, or should be, provided by someone else. This might happen where your husband had accepted your child as part of his family and is being sued for aliment. The child's father is also liable for aliment and the court would take this into account in fixing your husband's level of payments. Occasionally a child will have a substantial income of its own or, in the case of a grown-up child, could obtain a job. In these situations the court will usually not award any aliment for the child. The children's aliment is not usually affected if you live with another man (see p 56).

The past conduct or behaviour of the person claiming aliment is not taken into account in assessing how much to pay, unless it would be quite unjust to ignore it — if you had ill-treated your husband, for example.

You should try to agree informally with your husband or partner the amount of aliment payable for yourself and the children. Both of you can then ask the court to award this agreed amount instead of fighting lengthy and expensive legal proceedings. Moreover, an amount which has been agreed is more likely to be paid than one which has been "imposed" by the court.

Tactically when you and the children are seeking aliment, it may be better to concentrate on the aliment for the children. Aliment for children is often more willingly and reliably paid than aliment for wives. On the other hand, if the children are nearly grown-up their aliment will come to an end in a few years. You will then be left without support if you have concentrated on aliment for the children.

Your husband or partner can get tax relief on aliment paid to you and the children provided the aliment is paid in the correct way. This relief can make a considerable difference to the amount he can afford to pay. See Chapter 6 for further details.

The court will usually order him to pay a certain sum of aliment (monthly or weekly) starting from the date of making the order. You can ask the court to backdate the order to when you started proceedings or even earlier, but in the latter case, you must have a very good reason — your husband had left and you had only just traced him, for example.

DIVORCE

WHAT CAN I APPLY FOR?

If separation is followed by divorce, the court considers what new financial arrangements should be made. This is discussed in the following section.

When the court grants a decree of divorce it can make a variety of orders adjusting the financial position of you and your husband. The main orders are:—

- ordering you or your husband to pay a lump sum (called a 'capital sum') to the other;
- ordering you or your husband to pay the other a periodical allowance. This is a regular sum usually ordered to be paid weekly or monthly.
- ordering your husband to pay aliment for the children.

Other orders that can be made include a transfer of the tenancy of the home, transfer of the ownership of the home or other property, regulating the occupation of the home and varying any marriage settlement. Either you or your husband can apply for an order or orders; it doesn't matter which of you brings the divorce proceedings.

You and your husband should try to agree how the assets are to be divided and what periodical allowance and/or aliment is to be paid, and then ask the court to make the appropriate orders. Ask for what you need instead of making a large claim in the hope of ending up with a reasonable amount.

An agreed settlement is likely to be implemented, whereas court orders granted after bitter wrangles may well turn out to be unenforceable. Tactically it may be better to forgo periodical allowance for yourself and seek more aliment for the children; see p 49 on the advantages and disadvantages of this. Conciliation services now exist in some parts of Scotland to help couples to reach agreement about their finances and custody of the children (see p 3 for further details).

There is a new set of principles to guide the court in making orders on financial position. These are:—

- Family assets should be shared fairly between you and your husband; AND
- Account should be taken of economic advantages you derived from contributions made by your husband, and economic disadvantages you suffered in the interest of your husband or the family; your husband is treated similarly AND
- The economic burden of child care should be shared fairly; AND
- Where you or your husband has been financially dependent on the other during the marriage, support should be provided for up to three years; AND
- When divorce will cause serious financial hardship to you or your husband, provision should be made for you or him for a reasonable period.

Your or your husband's conduct will not be taken into account unless it was so bad it would be quite unjust to ignore it.

HOW THE COURT DECIDES WHAT TO DO

SHARING FAMILY ASSETS

These are to be shared equally unless there is a special reason for doing otherwise. Some examples of where an unequal division might be made are where the assets were bought with your or your family's money, or where your husband has a business (a farm for example) which cannot be divided and if sold would deprive him of a livelihood.

Family assets mean all the property and belongings you and your husband acquired during your marriage unless given by another person or inherited. Assets you and your husband acquired before marriage are not regarded as family assets. The only exceptions to this rule are the home and its contents. In so far as any of these items were bought before marriage for use by both of you after marriage they are treated as family assets.

ECONOMIC ADVANTAGES AND DISADVANTAGES

You will be entitled to have taken into account your contributions which have increased your husband's wealth. Your contributions may be financial or non-financial. For example you may have helped him build up his business, you may have worked to enable him to be trained, or you may have paid some of the bills for the home, done repairs or improvements or kept house. Your husband's contributions to your wealth are also taken into account.

Any economic disadvantages either of you suffered in the interest of the other or the family are also to be taken into account. For example, you may have given up your career in order to stay at home and look after the children, or he may not have taken a better job because you did not want to move away from your job.

FAIR SHARING OF CHILD CARE COSTS

If you are to look after the children after divorce, the court will take into account any loss of earnings you will suffer or the cost of employing someone to look after the children while you work, the cost of the extra accommodation necessary and the children's needs.

FINANCIAL DEPENDENCY

If you have been financially dependent on your husband you will be entitled to some financial provision to cushion you from the loss of this support after divorce. This support lasts for up to 3 years from the date of the divorce only, since it is designed to give you time to find a job or get training so you can support yourself.

SEVERE FINANCIAL HARDSHIP

Even where all the above factors have been taken into account you may be severely affected financially by divorce. For example, if you are an elderly wife who has never worked during a long marriage you will be entitled to financial provision for a reasonable period — the rest of your life perhaps. In assessing how much you need, the court looks at your age, health, earning capacity, how long you have been married and what standard of living you have enjoyed.

THE COURT'S ORDERS

On the basis of these principles the court makes an order or orders for your financial provision. It must first consider whether it is possible for your husband to provide for you solely by means of a lump sum and/or a transfer of property. For example, if you have no children the court may think that a modest lump sum to support you until you get back into employment, plus one half of the family assets would be sufficient.

But if you are looking after the children your provision will have to last for several years and your husband may not be able to afford to pay this in a lump sum. The court might order the lump sum to be paid in instalments. Alternatively, the court might transfer the house and furniture to you on the basis that you should then be able to support yourself and the children out of your earnings and the aliment you receive for the children.

Only if a lump sum and/or a transfer of property will not provide for you sufficiently can the court make a periodical allowance. Furthermore, you will have to demonstrate that a periodical allowance is justified on the grounds of fair sharing of child caring costs, or financial dependency or severe economic hardship (see p 52'). Your periodical allowance may be payable for an indefinite period, for a fixed number of years or until a specified event happens — the children leave home, for example.

You must apply for a lump sum or transfer of property order in the divorce proceedings; afterwards is too late. The lump sum can be ordered to be paid in instalments, or payment of it can be postponed. Similarly the date of transfer of property can be postponed. This could be useful where the property was the former matrimonial home. The court could for example leave you as the owner of the house until the children leave home, and then order you to transfer a half share of it to your husband.

Normally a claim for periodical allowance is made in the divorce proceedings. You can apply later but to be successful you will have to show that:
- there has been a change in circumstances since divorce; AND
- you did not waive your right to claim as part of the divorce settlement.

CHANGES IN MAINTENANCE
CAN THE AMOUNT BE CHANGED?
VOLUNTARY PAYMENTS

If your (ex)husband/partner is supporting you and/or the children by voluntary payments he can change the amount payable at any time. You would have to take legal proceedings for aliment or periodical allowance (but see p 46 and 53) if he refused to pay the amount you think he should be paying.

PAYMENTS UNDER ENFORCEABLE AGREEMENTS

Enforceable agreements usually provide for a change in the amount payable when circumstances change. The amount may, for instance, be calculated by reference to your and your (ex)husband's/partner's incomes, so that if you get an increase it will go down, but if he gets an increase it will go up. Similarly the children's aliment may be increased as they grow older.

Although you or your (ex)husband/partner can apply to the court for a variation of the agreement if dissatisfied with the increase or decrease provided for by the agreement, the court is unlikely to vary it as long as the agreement was fair and reasonable when it was prepared. Where a change of circumstances not covered by the agreement occurs you can either make a new agreement or, if you cannot agree, apply to the court for a variation of the amount payable. The agreement may contain a clause prohibiting application to the court. Whether this is effective depends on whether it was reasonable to put in such a clause when the agreement was made.

COURT ORDERS

If there has been a change in circumstances since the court awarded you and/or the children maintenance, either you or your (ex)husband/partner can go back to the court to ask for the amount to be varied.
For example if:
- he gets a better job; OR
- you lose your job or become part-time; OR
- you have additional dependants (such as other children) to support; OR
- the children need more money as they grow older,
the maintenance could be increased.

On the other hand if:
- you get a better job; OR
- he becomes unemployed; OR
- he has additional dependants (such as a new wife) to support; OR
- you are being supported by another man (see p 56); OR
- the children leave home,
your maintenance could be decreased or even terminated.

Inflation by itself may not justify an increase. The court would have to be satisfied that your (ex)husband/partner could afford to pay more since he would feel the effects of inflation too.

The court can backdate any variation to the date of the application or even to the date when the circumstances changed. This applies to any aliment, but only to your periodical allowance if it was awarded in proceedings started after 1 September 1986. Backdating is not allowed for periodical allowance awarded in proceedings started before then.

In the case of periodical allowance awarded in proceedings started after 1 September 1986 the court can, if asked, cancel your allowance and substitute an order requiring your ex-husband to pay you a lump sum and/or to transfer property to you. You might find this useful if your husband is not paying your periodical allowance regularly. Your ex-husband might prefer to pay you a lump sum (by instalments perhaps) rather than an allowance which could last for the remainder of your life. You should think carefully about substitution, however, because your ex-husband's income (and hence your periodical allowance) might well increase over the years. Once the court has made the substitution it cannot be changed back again.

Once these orders have been made they cannot normally be changed. All the court can do, if asked, is to alter the date of payment or transfer. For example if your ex-husband was ordered to pay you a lump sum, say one month after divorce, he could apply to pay it by instalments spread over a year or so. On the other hand if he was originally allowed to pay by instalments, you could ask the court to speed up the instalments or order that the outstanding balance be paid immediately. Similarly, either of you could ask the court to vary the date when an item of property is to be transferred.

LUMP SUM AND TRANSFER OF PROPERTY ORDERS

The court can cancel or vary a lump sum or transfer of property order on bankruptcy. If your ex-husband or wife:
- is made bankrupt within 5 years after the court order was made, AND
- the order made him or her insolvent — debts exceeded remaining assets,

the court may order you to repay or return all or part of the money or property. This is likely to be very uncommon. The divorce court is usually aware of a couple's financial circumstances and so would not have granted a lump sum or transfer of property order which made your ex-husband or wife insolvent.

WHAT HAPPENS IF MY PARTNER DIES?

ALIMENT

Your aliment and the children's aliment comes to an end automatically if your partner dies. Any arrears which were owing at the date of his death have to be paid out of his estate (money and property left by your late partner). You should tell his executors of your claim for arrears as soon as you can. You may be able to claim Child's Special Allowance (see p 65).

It is possible to apply to the court for an order requiring your late partner's executors to make an allowance out of his estate to replace your and/or the children's aliment. But these applications are most unusual as they are only possible if your partner left a great deal of money and you and/or the children did not get much under your partner's will or by way of legal rights (see p58).

PERIODICAL ALLOWANCE

Your periodical allowance, on the other hand, continues even after your ex-husband dies. His executors must continue to pay your allowance out of the estate and you can claim any arrears out of the estate. But his executors can (and will) apply to the court for an order cancelling your allowance. Normally this will be granted unless your ex-husband died well-off and you are in need of further support.

WHAT HAPPENS IF I COHABIT OR REMARRY?

If you live with another man your aliment or periodical allowance does not come to an end automatically. But your (ex) husband can apply to the court for it to be decreased or cancelled. Normally it will be cancelled if you are living with another man whether or not he is supporting you. But this is a "grey area" and practice varies.

If you remarry after divorce any periodical allowance payable ceases automatically. Your ex-husband remains liable to pay you any arrears which were owing at the date of your remarriage. You should tell your ex-husband of your remarriage as soon as it takes place, otherwise you may be faced with having to repay the instalments you received after remarriage in a lump sum.

The court will not generally alter the childrens' aliment if you remarry or live with another man unless he is supporting them to a substantial extent, or has accepted them as children of his family. Even in these cases their aliment payable by your ex-husband is likely to be decreased rather than cancelled.

WHAT HAPPENS IF MY PARTNER IS MADE BANKRUPT?

If your (ex)husband/partner was paying aliment or periodical allowance and is made bankrupt you can put in a claim for any arrears which were unpaid at the date of bankruptcy. You should notify your claim to the trustee who is appointed to sell the bankrupt's property for the benefit of all his creditors including you. You will probably be paid only a proportion of your claim; the remainder is written off.

The bankruptcy does not automatically terminate your aliment or periodical allowance and/or the children's aliment. However, the court, on application by your (ex)husband/partner, can cancel or reduce it for the future. Until this order is made, it is still due for the period after the start of his bankruptcy and you could enforce it if he ever has property or money of his own after the bankruptcy. See p 55 for the effect of bankruptcy on lump sum or transfer of property orders.

Aliment and periodical allowance are notoriously difficult to enforce because many people become reluctant payers once their relationships with their former families have cooled. Aliment for children is usually more regularly paid, which it is why it is often good tactics on splitting up to concentrate on claims for aliment for the children. Even if you know where your (ex)husband/partner is, the legal methods of enforcing payment (called diligence) are not very effective unless he is in steady employment or owns property or goods which can be sold. The DHSS may be able to help in tracing him — ask your solicitor to contact them if you wish to make use of their services.

ENFORCING YOUR MAINTENANCE

If your aliment or periodical allowance is contained in a court order or legally enforceable agreement and has not been paid you can:
- negotiate a payment plan with your (ex)husband/partner; OR
- claim Supplementary Benefit; OR
- use the legal methods of enforcing payment (called diligence) against him.

If you and your (ex)husband/partner are on reasonable terms with each other, you may be able to reach an agreement that the arrears are to be paid off by instalments in addition to regular payments of maintenance in future. If he has a bank account you can suggest that he should arrange for the payments to be made by standing order to ensure regularity.

If your total income including your aliment or periodical allowance is less than your Supplementary Benefit entitlement, you should claim benefit. The DHSS will take steps to recover from your partner the amount of money they have paid in benefit to you (except benefit paid for yourself after divorce) and/ or the children. See p63 for further details.

The main diligences used in Scotland are arrestment of your partner's pay or bank account, poinding and warrant sale of his goods, and civil imprisonment. All of these methods only recover arrears due at the date when diligence is done. They will not recover the future maintenance payments, although the threat of diligence may ensure that you are paid regularly in future. You will need a solicitor for diligence. If you were legally aided when you applied for the court order, your existing legal aid certificate covers the costs of diligence (except civil imprisonment) for up to 18 months after the date of the court order. After this you will have to apply for fresh legal aid (see Appendix 1). Civil imprisonment always requires a separate legal aid application.

If your partner lives in another part of the United Kingdom, a European Community country or certain other foreign countries, the courts there will help in enforcing payments due under your Scottish court order. You will need to get your solicitor in Scotland to take the appropriate action on your behalf.

YOUR INHERITANCE RIGHTS

Your inheritance rights on the death of your former partner depend on whether you were married to him or her and whether he or she left a will.

WHERE A WILL IS LEFT

If you and your partner are not married to each other you will inherit only what your partner leaves you by will or under a survivorship destination (see p 59).

If you and your husband or wife are still married to each other you are entitled to whatever he or she left you in the will. If the will leaves you nothing or only a small legacy you can claim "legal rights". Legal rights amount to half of your late husband's or wife's moveable property (roughly everything except buildings and land) if there are no children or descendants surviving, or one-third if there are. You have to choose between what (if anything) you are left in the will and your legal rights — you cannot have both.

If you are divorced you cannot claim legal rights from your ex-husband or wife. If he or she did not alter his or her will after divorce you may still be entitled to any legacy left to you, especially if you have been named rather than been described simply as "my wife" or "my husband". The law here is rather complex and you should seek independent legal advice if you think you have a claim.

WHERE NO WILL IS LEFT

If you were never married or are divorced, you are entitled to nothing if your partner or (ex)husband or wife does not leave a will. But if you are still married when your husband or wife dies you could end up inheriting most of his or her estate.

FIRST, you are entitled to the house (or share of the house) owned by your late husband or wife if:

- you were living in it when he or she died; AND
- it (or the share of it) is not worth more than £50,000; AND
- it is in Scotland; AND
- there is no survivorship destination (see below).

Where the house (or share of it) is worth more than £50,000 you get £50,000 in cash instead. But you may be able to buy the house from the estate by making up the difference yourself. You may only get the value (up to £50,000) if the house forms part of a larger property used for buiness purposes — a farmhouse on a farm for example.

You will normally be entitled to take over your late husband's or wife's tenancy if you were living in the house before the death. You should contact the landlord as soon as possible to let them know what you intend to do.

SECONDLY, you get the furniture and contents owned by your late husband or wife up to £10,000 in value and a cash sum of up to either £15,000 or £25,000. The larger sum is due if your late husband or wife leaves no surviving children or descendants.

THIRDLY, you get one third of any remaining moveable property (roughly everything except buildings and land) if your late husband or wife leaves children or other descendants. If there are no children or descendants surviving you get one half.

FINALLY, if your late husband or wife is not survived by any descendants, brothers/sisters or their descendants, or parents, you will inherit the whole of the estate.

SURVIVORSHIP DESTINATIONS

When a couple buy a home together the title is frequently taken in such a way that the whole property passes to the survivor on the death of one of the couple. In this case you will inherit the home on your partner's death as long as:

- the title has not been altered after you separated or divorced; AND
- your partner has not left his or her share to someone else by will.

Whether your partner is entitled to leave his or her share by will to someone else depends on how the home was paid for. Generally, if you helped pay for the home your partner cannot leave his or her share by will to someone else.

YOUR RIGHTS UNDER YOUR PARTNER'S PENSION SCHEME

Private pension schemes for employed or self-employed people generally provide for a pension to be paid to widows. Some schemes also provide for pensions to widowers who were financially dependant on their wives. Schemes do not normally provide for a pension to be paid to an unmarried partner, but you may be able to make a claim if you are looking after your late partner's children, so it is always worth getting into contact with the managers of the scheme.

Many pension schemes for employed people provide for a lump sum to be paid to the scheme member's estate if he or she dies before retirement. Rather than have this sum form part of the estate, some schemes allow members to nominate who is to receive it on his or her death. The usual person nominated is a wife or husband and in this case nomination is automatically cancelled by divorce. If you are not married you could consider asking the managers of the scheme whether your partner can nominate you.

These rights to a dependant's pension and/or a lump sum can be very valuable especially in the case of elderly people. You will lose your rights to both on divorce, so you should make sure that your loss of these future rights is taken into account in your divorce settlement. See p 99 for how divorce can affect your state retirement pension.

MONEY AND THE STATE

This chapter looks at the various state welfare benefits to which you may be entitled after splitting up and how your and your partner's incomes are taxed then.

SUPPLEMENTARY BENEFIT
SINGLE PAYMENTS
FAMILY INCOME SUPPLEMENT
HOUSING BENEFIT
CHILD BENEFIT AND ONE PARENT BENEFIT
CHILD'S SPECIAL ALLOWANCE
EDUCATION BENEFITS
NATIONAL HEALTH SERVICE BENEFITS

WELFARE BENEFITS

HOW SPLITTING UP AFFECTS YOUR INCOME TAX
HOW YOUR MAINTENANCE IS TAXED
HOW A CHILD'S ALIMENT IS TAXED
TAX RELIEF ON HOME LOANS
OTHER WAYS OF SAVING TAX

INCOME TAX

CAPITAL GAINS TAX

WELFARE BENEFITS

Major changes to the state benefit system are planned for April 1988. Supplementary Benefit, Family Income Supplement and Single Payments are to be replaced by Income Support, Family Credit and Social Fund Payments. Child's Special Allowance is to be abolished. This book gives brief details of the benefits available at the date of publication. You should check the current position with your local Citizens Advice Bureau or DHSS office.

SUPPLEMENTARY BENEFIT

This is the main benefit for people with little or no money of their own. It is means tested, so you will only get it if your income is below a certain amount. The amount changes every year and depends on your circumstances.

You cannot claim benefit if you or your partner have a job but you may be able to claim Family Income Supplement instead (see p 64).

You cannot claim if you have more than £3,000 in savings (1986/87 figure). Savings include cash, money in the bank or building society, national savings certificates, stocks, shares, and may also include any life policy which can be given up for cash (disregarding the first £1,500). Your home, your furniture and personal possessions do not count as savings unless you have particularly valuable furniture or personal possessions. The way a lump sum payable on divorce, a lump sum payment of arrears of maintenance or cash from the sale of the former family home is treated is complex — depending on the circumstances it may be treated as savings or as income spread out over a number of weeks.

If you remarry your and your husband's or wife's entitlement to benefit will be reassessed by the DHSS. Living with a new partner will usually affect your (and your partner's) entitlement, but it does depend on the nature of your relationship. Seek further advice if you are unsure of your position.

HOW TO CLAIM

You claim by filling in a form which you get from your local DHSS office, or if you are registered as unemployed, your unemployment benefit office. Someone from your local DHSS office may interview you at home to get full details of your financial position. It is unwise to make false statements in order to get benefit. If you are found out you will have to repay it and may be prosecuted as well.

Any maintenance payments you and/or the children living with you receive counts as income in working out how much benefit (if any) you are due. You should contact your local DHSS office promptly if your maintenance stops or is delayed, so that your benefit can be adjusted.

If maintenance is paid irregularly the DHSS may:
- pay you benefit regularly as if no maintenance was payable. You will have to hand over any maintenance you actually receive; OR
- make you claim benefit every week. The amount you get each week will depend on whether or not maintenance was paid.

You are not obliged to take legal proceedings to get maintenance or to enforce the court order you have got before you can claim benefit. The DHSS will suggest that you take action, but they are not entitled to refuse benefit if you say no. You should appeal at once if benefit is refused on this ground.

For Supplementary benefit purposes a husband and wife are equally liable to maintain each other and both parents are equally liable to maintain their children. These people are called 'liable relatives'. Neither cohabiting partners nor divorced husbands or wives are liable to maintain each other.

If you claim benefit after splitting up, you will be asked for details of any relative liable to maintain you or any children for whom you are claiming (your husband or the children's father, for instance). The DHSS will contact any 'liable relative' in order to investigate his or her financial position. If they think that he or she should be paying maintenance or more maintenance, they will request him or her to do so. A liable relative who refuses may be prosecuted and, on being found guilty, fined or imprisoned. Alternatively the DHSS may apply to the court for an order requiring the liable relative to pay them such a sum (up to the amount of benefit provided) as the court thinks reasonable.

The DHSS have different rules from the court for working out how much maintenance ought to be paid. This means that sometimes a liable relative will be required to pay more than the amount in the court order.

HOW MAINTENANCE AFFECTS YOUR BENEFIT

SINGLE PAYMENTS

To get a Single Payment you must be either on Supplementary benefit or eligible for benefit. These payments are meant for special "one-off" needs, not normal living expenses. For example, you may be able to get money for:

- a cot, pram, nappies etc. for a new baby;
- funeral expenses of a close relative who left no money to pay them;
- clothes, if they are destroyed or stolen;
- essential household furniture, if you move out because of violence or breakdown of marriage and you can't get furnished accommodation;
- removal costs, if you have to move house;
- travelling to see your child who is living with the other parent where custody has not been decided;
- essential repairs to your house, unless someone else (the landlord for example) is legally bound to do them;
- rent in advance or a deposit.

You must claim before you buy what you need; otherwise your claim will be rejected. In your claim you will have to say why you need a Single Payment. If you have more than £500 (1986/87 figure) in savings your Single Payment will be reduced by the excess. This may mean you get nothing. If the DHSS thinks you could get hold of the item more cheaply — a secondhand pram or furniture for example — you will only get that amount, and if they think you don't really need the item at all or you could borrow it, your claim will be refused.

FAMILY INCOME SUPPLEMENT

Family Income Supplement is a benefit to boost the income of low paid workers who are bringing up at least one dependant child.

The amount you will get depends on your income and savings and the number and ages of children. If you are living with your husband, wife or a partner, his or her income and savings is added to yours to see whether you qualify.

It is worth claiming Family Income Supplement, even if the amount you get is small, as it is a "passport" to many other benefits such as free school meals and prescriptions.

HOUSING BENEFIT

Housing Benefit helps you pay your rent and/or rates. The amount of benefit you will get depends on how much rent and/or rates you pay and what your income and needs are. If you are living with your husband, wife or partner, his or her income and needs are counted in with yours to see whether you qualify, and if so how much you are entitled to. If there are people living in your household who are not dependent on you, the amount of Housing benefit you are entitled to may be affected as they may be expected to contribute to your rent and/or rates. Your local social security office or district/islands council will advise you.

Housing benefit is claimed from your local district/islands council even if you are paying rent to a private landlord. But if you are already on Supplementary Benefit, you do not need to claim Housing Benefit separately, because the DHSS will organise payment by your council directly to you.

Child Benefit is a tax free benefit paid to persons bringing up children. Your income is not taken into account — you can get child benefit however well off you are.

CHILD BENEFIT AND ONE PARENT BENEFIT

You can claim Child Benefit if you are bringing up a child who is under 16, or if the child is still at school or in full-time education, under 19. If the child is not living with you, you must be paying the person looking after him or her at least as much as the Child Benefit. Normally the person the child is living with will claim benefit and has priority over you. The rate of Child Benefit for 1986/87 is £7.10 per week.

One Parent Benefit is an addition (£4.60 per week in 1986/87) to Child Benefit payable to people bringing up children alone. You can claim if:—
● you are getting Child Benefit; AND
● you are single, widowed, separated or divorced.

If you are married you must have been separated from your partner for at least 13 weeks before you are entitled to One Parent Benefit. This extra benefit is stopped if you remarry or cohabit. If you are already getting an increase for children with a widow's pension or allowance you are not entitled to One Parent Benefit.

You can get this allowance if:—
● you are looking after a child who is under 16, or, if the child is still at school or in full-time education, under 19; AND
● you are divorced; AND
● you have not remarried and are not cohabiting; AND

CHILD'S SPECIAL ALLOWANCE

- your former husband paid maintenance (or was bound under a court order or agreement to pay maintenance) for the child, and has died.

You should claim within 3 months of your former husband's death, as your allowance will not normally be backdated more than this. Though you cannot get both One Parent Benefit and a Child's Special Allowance you should claim the allowance as it is worth more, £8.05 as against £4.60 for One Parent Benefit (1986/87 figures).

EDUCATION BENEFITS

Your children may be eligible for free school meals, free transport to and from school, and an allowance for school clothes if your income is low. Grants for higher education are also available. Ask at the Education Department of your Regional Council if you think you might be entitled to any of these benefits.

NATIONAL HEALTH SERVICE BENEFITS

You may be able to get help with optical, dental and prescription charges if your income is low. Further details are available from the optician, dentist, doctor, chemist or DHSS office.

INCOME TAX
HOW SPLITTING UP AFFECTS YOUR POSITION

COHABITING COUPLES

The incomes of a cohabiting couple are not lumped together nor can a married man's allowance be claimed by the man, although an additional personal allowance can be claimed by either parent if there are children. Each of you was liable for tax on your own income while you lived together, so that splitting up by itself normally has no effect on your and your partner's tax position.

MARRIED COUPLES

In the case of a married couple the husband's and the wife's incomes are usually lumped together and tax is charged on the combined incomes. A married man's allowance (£3,665 in 1986/87) can be deducted from the combined incomes in working out the taxable income (the income on which tax is charged), and an allowance called wife's earned income relief (£2,335 in 1986/87) is also available to deduct from any earned income of the wife.

EXAMPLE 1: Married couple living together.

Ian's income	£6,000	
Margaret's income (earned)	£6,000	
Total Income		£12,000
Married allowance	£3,665	
Wife's earned income relief	£2,335	
Total Tax Free Income		£6,000
Taxable income		£6,000
Tax at 29%		£1,740

A couple can choose to have the wife's earned income taxed separately; but both must be well paid before this will save money.

After a married couple split up each person has to look after his or her own tax affairs and is taxed only on his or her own income. Each can claim at least a single person's allowance. A person who has a child or children living with them for the whole tax year can claim an additional personal allowance (£1,330 in 1986/87). Any child must be under 16, unless he or she is in full-time education or training. A man whose separated wife is maintained wholly by payments made by him can continue to claim a married man's allowance to set against his income, but cannot claim an additional personal allowance as well.

EXAMPLE 2: Separated or divorced couple.

IAN		MARGARET	
Income	£6,000	Income	£6,000
Personal allowance	£2,335	Personal allowance	£2,335
Taxable income	£3,665	Taxable income	£3,665
Tax at 29% payable by Ian	£1,062.85	Tax at 29% payable by Margaret	£1,062.85

There are special rules for the tax year in which a married couple separate. The husband is liable to tax on his income for the whole of the tax year together with his wife's income from the start of the tax year (6th April) to the date of separation. Against this he can set a married man's allowance and wife's earned income relief (except where the couple have opted to have the wife's earnings taxed separately) together with any other reliefs to which he may be entitled. The wife is liable to tax on her own income from the date of separation to the end of the tax year. Against this she can set a single personal allowance and any other reliefs to which she may be entitled (such as an additional personal allowance if she has a child or children living with her).

EXAMPLE 3: Married couple in the year of separation.
Ian and Margaret separate on 5th October — half way through the tax year.

IAN			MARGARET	
Own income for whole year		£6,000	Income (earned)	
Margaret's income (earned)			from 6th October	
from 6th April – 5th October		£3,000	– 5th April	£3,000
Total Income		£9,000		
Married man's allowance	£3,665		Personal allowance	£2,335
Wife's earned income relief	£2,335		Taxable income	£665
Total Tax Free Income		£6,000		
Taxable income		£3,000	Tax at 29% payable	
			by Margaret	£192.85
Tax at 29% payable by Ian		£870		

You and your husband or wife should tell your tax offices as soon as you split up so that your tax position can be reviewed. Delay may mean that you pay too much tax. This can take some time to reclaim.

If you and your husband or wife are reconciled in the tax year in which you separated you are treated as never having separated. Both of you should inform your tax offices of any reconciliation.

HOW YOUR MAINTENANCE IS TAXED

The way your maintenance (aliment or periodical allowance) is treated for tax purposes depends on:
- whether it is paid voluntarily, under a court order or under an enforceable agreement; AND
- how much maintenance is being paid.

For simplicity the following sections are written from the viewpoint of a woman receiving maintenance from her (ex) husband or partner.

VOLUNTARY PAYMENTS

If your husband or partner gives you money when you split up without any enforceable agreement or court order having been made, these voluntary payments are treated as gifts. They do not count as part of your income, but on the other hand your husband or partner cannot deduct the amount he pays from his income when working out his taxable income. As long as you are being wholly maintained by these voluntary payments, your husband (but not your partner) can continue to claim a married man's allowance until divorce. After divorce, however, he can no longer claim a married man's allowance.

ENFORCEABLE AGREEMENTS

The maintenance you receive is part of your income and you must include it in your tax return. Your husband or partner can deduct the amount he pays from his income in working out his taxable income.

If maintenance is paid under an enforceable agreement your husband deducts tax at the basic rate (29% in 1986/87) from each payment before he sends it to you. For example, if you get £200 per month he will deduct £58 in tax and pay you the balance of £142. Unless you are so well off that you are paying higher rates of tax (starting at taxable incomes over £17,200 per year in 1986/87) you will not have to pay any further income tax on your maintenance. If you are not well off, you may be able to reclaim all or part of the tax which your husband deducted before he paid you.

To reclaim, write to your tax office with details of your total income and allowances and a statement from your husband showing how much he has paid and how much tax he has deducted. He is obliged to give you this statement if you ask for it. To save you waiting till the end of the year for your tax refund, you can arrange with your tax office to have the refund paid by instalments at regular intervals throughout the year.

The person paying maintenance under an enforceable agreement must remember to deduct tax at 29% from each payment, otherwise the tax office may refuse to give any tax relief on the payments later. The amount of maintenance paid before deducting tax (£200 per month in the example above) should be shown in the person's tax return. Only what was actually paid — not what you should have been paid under the agreement but wasn't — should be shown. Overstating the amount paid is treated as a serious tax offence. Depending on how much income the person paying maintenance has, he may be entitled to more tax relief, or may have to pay the Inland Revenue part of the tax already deducted from the maintenance payments.

EXAMPLE 4: Maintenance payments under an agreement.

James earns £10,000 per year. He is due to pay his wife Janet £200 per month under an enforceable agreement. James actually pays £142 per month and retains £58 as tax relief.

JAMES			JANET	
Income		£10,000	Income (maintenance)	£2,400
Personal allowance	£2,335		Personal allowance	£2,335
Maintenance paid	£2,400		Taxable income	£65
Total Tax allowance		£4,735		
Taxable income		£5,265		

James has deducted £696 tax (12 x £58) from Janet's maintenance over the year. Janet is only due to pay £18.85 in tax (29% of £65). She will be able to reclaim £677.15 (£696 — £18.85) from her tax office.

COURT ORDERS

The maintenance you receive under a court order is part of your income, and you must include it in your tax return. Your husband or partner can deduct the amount he pays from his income in working out his taxable income. Where the amount is more than the SMALL MAINTENANCE PAYMENT limits (the figures for 1986/87 are £48 per week or £208 per month for your maintenance, £48 per week or £208 per month for maintenance for a child payable directly to him or her, and £25 per week or £108 per month for a child if payable to you for his or her benefit) it is paid in exactly the same way as for enforceable agreements — tax at 29% is deducted from each payment and only the balance paid over (see p 69). But maintenance not in excess of the limits, "a small maintenance payment", is paid in full without deduction of tax, so that you receive the full amount the court has ordered to be paid. Depending on how much other income you may have, you may have to pay tax on your maintenance. If you are employed, your PAYE code will be altered to take account of the maintenance you are receiving. If you are not employed, any tax due is payable as a lump sum so you should remember to put money aside to meet this.

EXAMPLE 5: Small maintenance payments under a court order.

Alexander earns £5,000 per year. He is due to pay his ex-wife Margaret £100 per month under a court order. Margaret has no other income. Alexander pays Margaret £100 per month in full as it is a small maintenance payment.

ALEXANDER			MARGARET	
Income		£5,000	Income (maintenance)	£1,200
Personal allowance	£2,335		Personal allowance	£2,335
Maintenance paid	£1,200		Taxable income	NIL
Total Tax allowance		£3,535		
Taxable income		£1,465		

Margaret does not have to pay any tax on her maintenance.

HOW A CHILD'S ALIMENT IS TAXED

If the court orders your husband to pay aliment for the children living with you it can either order the payments to be made to you for their support or it can order the payments to be made to the children directly, although the money is in fact payable to you as their guardian. Substantial amounts of tax may be saved by asking the court to make the latter type of order (see Examples 6A and 6B below). Where all the maintenance is payable to you (for yourself and the children) it all counts as your income, but where the children's aliment is awarded to them it counts as their income, so that their personal allowances can be set against it.

You can also save tax in this way if the payments are made under an enforceable agreement as long as the agreement is "registered for execution" in the court registers — either a national register at Edinburgh called the Books of Council and Session or registers kept at each sheriff court. Registered for execution means that the agreement can be enforced without having to go to court. An agreement cannot be registered for execution unless this is part of the agreement. Tax can be saved in this way only where you and your husband or partner are living apart.

this is part of the agreement. Tax can be saved in this way only where you and your husband or partner are living apart.

EXAMPLE 6: Children's aliment.

William pays a total of £400 per month for his wife Elizabeth and the two children Peter and Lucy under a court order. They have no other income.

A. If whole amount is awarded to Elizabeth for support of herself and the children

ELIZABETH

Income		£4,800
Personal allowance	£2,335	
Additional Personal allowance	£1,330	
Total Tax Free allowance		£3,665
Taxable income		£1,135

Tax at 29% payable by Elizabeth £329.15

B. If £200 per month is awarded to Elizabeth and £100 per month directly to each of the children.

ELIZABETH

Income		£2,400
Personal allowance	£2,335	
Additional personal allowance	£1,330	
Total Tax Free allowance		£3,665
Taxable Income		NIL

LUCY/PETER

Income	£1,200
Personal allowance	£2,335
Net taxable income	NIL

By asking the court to award the children's aliment to them directly £329.15 has been saved.

It makes no difference to the tax position of the person paying the children's aliment which way it is paid. If you have already got a court order awarding you maintenance for yourself and the children, you can go back to the court for the order to be varied so that the children's aliment is awarded directly to them. The court will usually grant such a variation, but it will not divide your own maintenance among the children as well.

If the aliment is being paid under an enforceable agreement you and your partner could make a new agreement in which the children's aliment is payable to them.

TAX RELIEF ON HOME LOANS

While a married couple live together interest paid on a loan of not more than £30,000 can be deducted in working out taxable income, provided the loan has been used for the purchase or improvement of their home. On separation or divorce each of you is eligible for relief on a loan of up to £30,000 used to buy yourselves separate accommodation.

There are certain situations where relief is not given on interest paid so that you should try to avoid them.
- If you are living in the home which is owned by your husband or wife and he or she pays the interest, tax relief is available. This is still true after the divorce. But if you pay the interest there is no relief, although practice varies and some tax offices will allow it.
- You may want to buy another home with the help of a loan for your wife or husband to live in. You will not get any tax relief on loan interest you pay for that home. It is better to pay increased maintenance (on which you get tax relief) so that your wife or husband can take out a loan and pay the interest (which is eligible for tax relief) themselves.
- When part of the financial settlement is that you pay your husband or wife a lump sum, you may have to obtain a loan or additional loan on the security of the home to raise the money. You will get relief if the home was partly owned by your husband or wife and it is clear that the lump sum is buying out his or her share. You are unlikely to get tax relief if the home is in your name alone, although you could argue that you were buying out your husband's or wife's occupancy rights. To support this argument you should have an agreement prepared stating this and containing a renunciation of occupancy rights.
- Cohabiting partners each qualify for tax relief on interest paid on a loan of not more than £30,000 or a joint loan of not more than £60,000. Where

one partner owns the home and moves out after splitting up, interest paid by the absent owner no longer qualifies for relief.

OTHER WAYS OF SAVING TAX

If the children are at private schools the parent paying aliment for them may be able to arrange that the fees count as the childrens' income. You should get advice from a solicitor, accountant or the school on a suitable scheme.

You should avoid paying bills (such as rent, rates, fuel bills or clothes) for your partner or the children. It is better to increase their maintenance so that they can pay the bills themselves. You will get tax relief on the increased maintenance, but they may not have to pay more tax on the extra they receive.

CAPITAL GAINS TAX

There is no tax payable on any assets transferred between husband and wives while they are living together or in the tax year in which they separate. Assets transferred thereafter may result in tax being charged. But there are exemptions for the home and the first £6,300 (1986/87 figure) of any "gain" (the value of the asset at the date of transfer or sale less its value after allowing for inflation at the date you acquired it) in a tax year is also exempt. You should seek professional advice from a solicitor or an accountant if you think you may be liable.

ARRANGEMENTS FOR THE CHILDREN

This chapter deals with the different arrangements that can be made for the children, and the legal position regarding custody, guardianship and access when you and your partner split up.

CUSTODY

GUARDIANSHIP

ACCESS

When you split up you and your partner will have to decide what is to happen to the children. Splitting up can be very difficult for children to cope with. Their home is broken up, they may have to leave their familiar surroundings and their friends, and they will be faced with the pressures of conflicting loyalties to each parent. Try to explain to the children about the splitting up and what is going to happen to them. They are probably more confused and upset than you realise and need to have someone to talk over their concerns with. By considering the children's needs you and your partner can help them to come through the process of splitting up relatively unscathed.

There is a temptation to use the children as a means of getting at your partner — by contesting custody or refusing access for instance. Whatever else you disagree about, you should try to agree about the arrangements to be made for the children. Don't forget about the children's wishes — involve them in the discussions if they are old enough. Various counselling agencies are available to help you and your partner reach a mutually acceptable solution - see Chapter 1 for further details.

CUSTODY

During marriage each parent has joint custody, but on splitting up one parent will usually apply for and be granted sole custody. Where the parents are not married, the mother normally has sole custody while she lives with the father and retains sole custody on splitting up.

One parent having sole custody on splitting up is the normal situation; other options are listed on p77.

SOLE CUSTODY

If you have sole custody of the children then (unless a court or children's hearing has ordered otherwise) you are entitled to: —
- have the children living with you. But you must not take them out of Scotland permanently or change their nationality without the consent of the other parent (an unmarried father's consent is not required) or the court.
- have day-to-day care of the children.
- make day-to-day decisions regarding the children.

You have duties — to provide a home for the children, to look after them properly, and to see that they receive suitable education and medical treatment.

Your husband or wife as the non-custodian parent retains certain rights. For example he or she can consent to medical treatment for the child. See p80 for a parent's rights as guardian.

The way in which you exercise your rights and fulfill your duties as the parent with sole custody may be challenged by the other parent or some outside body, such as the local authority, applying to the court. Your views will not automatically prevail as the court decides such disputes on the basis of what is best for the children. By and large the court will not interfere unless your actions are shown to be harming the children. Your partner may also apply for custody to be transferred to him or her.

Most children benefit from contact with both their parents. Even though you have sole custody you should try not to shut their other parent out from the children's lives and decisions about them. See p81 for access by their other parent.

OTHER CUSTODY ARRANGEMENTS

Apart from one parent having sole custody other arrangements can be made for the children on splitting up. These are less common:

- joint custody. You and the other parent can both have custody although the children are in your care. Joint custody preserves both parents' roles in bringing up the children. On the other hand each of you has equal rights and so is equally entitled to take any step concerning the children. Joint custody will only work well if you and the other parent co-operate with each other and he or she does not interfere with your day-to-day care of the children.
- a relative, such as a grandparent, having custody. This might be done if you and the other parent were planning to lead unsettled lives (working abroad on short-term contracts for example)
- placing the children in the care of, or under the supervision of, the local authority. This is rare as it is only done where the court considers both parents are unsuitable to have custody.
- split custody and care. Here the court awards one parent sole custody but the children live with and are cared for by their other parent. This is very uncommon.

SPLITTING UP THE CHILDREN

Instead of one parent having custody of and looking after all the children, each of you could look after some. As a general rule it is better not to split up young children and the courts are reluctant to make such orders. If the children are split up remember that they need to keep in touch with each other and arrange visits, letters or telephone calls if you can.

CUSTODY OF STEP CHILDREN

You do not have custody of your step-children (your husband's or wife's children by a former marriage) simply because you are married to their parent. If you want custody of them (either solely or jointly) you will have to apply to the court.

Where you and your husband or wife have jointly adopted his or her children (your step-children) you will have joint custody automatically. But there is a trend against adoption by a step-parent nowadays if the children's other parent is alive as adoption cuts all legal ties between the children and the other parent.

HOW TO GET CUSTODY

Married parents have joint custody of their children automatically. This means that if one parent wishes sole custody he or she has to apply to the court.

In the case of unmarried parents the mother has sole custody, so that the father has to apply to the court if he wishes sole or joint custody of his children.

You can apply to the court for custody either as part of the separation or divorce proceedings or in independent proceedings. If you want to get custody as soon as you and your partner separate, perhaps to prevent your partner interfering with or removing the children or to strengthen your position in case custody disputes arise later, you would be best to go for custody independently of any separation or divorce action. You may need to get sole custody in order to obtain accommodation for yourself and the children. Some local authorities insist on a custody order before accepting you onto their housing waiting list or providing you with accommodation.

Many couples, however, are content to leave formal regulation of custody until a separation or divorce action is brought. As soon as such an action is started an application can be made for INTERIM CUSTODY. This will last until the separation or divorce action is heard, at which time the court will consider the question of custody again. The court tends not to change custody because of the unsettling effect on the children. So if you do not wish your husband or wife to end up having custody, you would be well advised not to leave home without the children and to challenge any claim for interim custody or apply for interim custody yourself.

Sometimes the parent looking after the children does not bother to ask the court for custody. This usually happens where the other parent has disappeared or shows no interest in the children.

If there is a dispute over custody between you and your partner, the court decides on the basis of what is best for the children, looking at their long term interests.
The factors it takes into account include:
- What sort of home each of you could offer; AND
- How much personal attention each of you would give the children; AND
- The conduct and character of you and your partner and any new partner either of you has; AND

- The likely stability of any new relationship which you or your partner have formed; AND
- Whether the children should be moved; AND
- The views of the children.

To help it decide who is to have custody, the court may appoint a person — usually an advocate or a social worker — to prepare an independent report on the situation. This person will interview you and your partner, any new partner either of you has, and look at the accommodation that would be provided for the children in each case. He or she may also interview neighbours, relatives, teachers at school and doctors. Neither the mother nor the father has a better claim to custody, but in practice courts are very reluctant to give custody of young children to their father against the wishes of their mother. The court is also unwilling to disturb the children unnecessarily. So if the children have been living with you since the separation, the court will tend to award custody to you in the event of a dispute.

The views of older children as to which parent they would prefer to live are very important. Custody of a child over 12 will not usually be awarded to one parent if the child strongly prefers to live with the other parent. Some judges interview the children in private to find out their views on the arrangements proposed for them.

ENFORCING YOUR CUSTODY RIGHTS

If you have custody you are entitled to have the children living with you, unless a court or a children's hearing has ordered that they should live elsewhere.

If the person holding the children refuses to hand them over to you, you will have to go to court for an order requiring the person to deliver them to you. Failure to obey such a delivery order is a contempt of court and the person can be fined or imprisoned. The court may also authorise a sheriff officer to search for the children and hand them over to you.

See p14 for what to do if you fear that the children will be taken out of the United Kingdom against your wishes or "snatched" from your custody.

HOW LONG DOES A CUSTODY ORDER LAST?

A custody order is not final; it can be changed later if the circumstances change. For example, if you have acquired a suitable home, or remarried, or now have a job which doesn't mean you have to go abroad frequently, you could apply to the court for the children to be transferred to your custody. The court is, however, normally reluctant to shunt children around. Before ordering a change of custody it would have to be satisfied that your new situation is likely to be permanent, and that there would be long term advantages to the children in the transfer.

Custody orders may end when the child reaches 16; but the law is not clear. If the order does end, both parents would have joint custody again if they were or had been married, while in the case of unmarried parents the mother regains her sole custody. In practice custody is almost impossible to enforce if a 16 or 17 year old decides to live elsewhere. Custody orders certainly end at 18. When children reach this age they can live wherever they like and are free of all parental control.

GUARDIANSHIP
WHAT IS GUARDIANSHIP?

A guardian's role is to act on behalf of a child in legal and property matters. Where the child is under 14 (boys) or 12 (girls) a guardian has to act for them in legal proceedings and deal with their property. Above these ages and until they are 18 the guardian has to agree to any legal actions or important financial arrangements which they may wish to make. A guardian has other rights and duties. For example, his or her agreement to the child's adoption is required, and his or her views as to the child's education must be taken into account.

GUARDIANSHIP OF YOUR CHILDREN

A married couple are the joint guardians of their children. Either can take action concerning the children without consulting the other. Any outsider or organisation can rely on instructions or authority given by either joint guardian, but they may refuse to act on one joint guardian's instructions if they are aware that the other objects.

If you and your husband or wife cannot agree over some aspect of guardianship, either can apply to the court to resolve the dispute. The court will decide on the basis of what would be in the best interests of the child.

When you and your husband or wife split up both of you remain joint guardians. It is very uncommon for a parent to be deprived of guardianship of his or her children. But this could happen if one parent was awarded sole custody and the other persistently interfered with the children's upbringing, or if the local authority assumed parental rights.

For unmarried parents the position is different. The mother is the sole guardian. The father would have to apply to the court to be appointed as a guardian either solely or jointly with her.

ACCESS
CAN I SEE
THE CHILDREN?

When you and your partner split up your rights to see the children (called access rights) depend on:
* informal arrangements made with your partner; OR
* what the court has ordered.

The parent with sole custody has the right to control access but is expected to allow you a reasonable degree of access. If you feel that your access is being unreasonably limited, you can apply to the court for an order setting out what access you are to have.

While you and your partner have joint custody, your rights of access are not limited. However if you disrupt the children's life too much by demanding to see them at unreasonable hours, your partner may decide to apply to the court for restriction of your access, and perhaps sole custody too.

Where access is awarded by the court it states how and when access is to take place — visiting every Sunday afternoon between 2 and 6 or having the children to stay for a week every school holidays for example. The court can order supervised access — access only in the presence of another person — if it is concerned for the children's safety or possible non-return.

You and your partner should think about and discuss what sort of access arrangements would be best for you and the children. Remember to involve the children in your discussions if they are old enough. Counselling and conciliation services (see Chapter 1) are available to help find an arrangement acceptable to all of you. The arrangement need not be rigid — for example you could be allowed to come and see the children whenever it was convenient.

As a means of keeping in contact, having the children to stay with you over a weekend or during part of the holidays may be better than visiting them in your partner's home or taking them out for a few hours. An outing every Sunday afternoon can turn into a chore for you and the children instead of being something to look forward to. Different ages of children need different types of arrangement. An older child will appreciate some individual contact with you rather than always seeing you with younger brothers or sisters.

Access may well be upsetting for both of you and the children just after the split up. Maintaining contact with both parents during this difficult period is important for the children, because once contact is lost it is not easy to re-establish. If you cannot see the children you may be able to keep in touch in other ways, such as telephoning, letters or occasional presents. Getting information about their progress from the school will also help you to feel involved.

It is unwise for you to set the children against their other parent. If he or she has been awarded access you have a duty to encourage the children to see or go with him or her unless you are convinced that this would be bad for them. If you are the parent who has access you should not question the children too closely about their home life as the other might resent it as prying.

Where you and your partner cannot agree about access, either of you can apply to the court for an order regulating access. The court will decide on the basis of what is in the best interests of the children. It is generally thought to be in their best interests to keep in touch with both parents. Access will not be imposed on older children against their wishes. Access would also be refused to a parent leading a dissolute life or likely to hurt the children. One situation that creates difficulties is where a woman who separated because of her partner's violence is afraid to allow him access because he might trace her through the children. Practice varies as to whether access will be refused on this ground.

Other people, grandparents for example, may wish to see the children. If this cannot be agreed the court can be asked to order that access be given.

If the court has granted you access and your partner continues to refuse to allow you to see the children in terms of the order you can report this to the court. He or she will normally be asked to attend court, so that the judge can explain the serious consequence of refusing to obey the court order. Refusal to obey a court order is contempt of court which can be punished by a fine or imprisonment. Another course of action the court can take if your partner persistently refuses you access is to give you custody instead, although it is usually very reluctant to take such a drastic step.

PROBLEMS WITH ACCESS ORDERS

GETTING DIVORCED

This chapter looks at the legal proceedings involved in getting divorced.

CAN I GET DIVORCED IN SCOTLAND?

WHICH COURT?

ADULTERY
BEHAVIOUR
DESERTION
NON-COHABITATION

GROUNDS FOR DIVORCE

DIY DIVORCE

STARTING THE ACTION
INTERIM ORDERS
CONTESTED ACTIONS
RECONCILIATION
AFFIDAVIT EVIDENCE
CUSTODY
GRANTING THE DIVORCE
NOTIFICATION OF DIVORCE

ORDINARY DIVORCE PROCEDURE

DIY DIVORCES
ORDINARY DIVORCE PROCEEDURE
LEGAL AID FUND'S CHARGE

WHAT WILL IT COST?

CAN I GET DIVORCED IN SCOTLAND?

You can get divorced in Scotland if:—
- You or your husband or wife are domiciled in Scotland — meaning Scotland is regarded as your permanent home — at the date of bringing the action; OR
- You or your husband or wife have been habitually resident in Scotland for at least a year before bringing the action.

The rules for bringing actions in England and Wales are very similar. So if you are domiciled in Scotland and your husband or wife is domiciled in England or Wales you have a choice. You can bring your divorce action either in Scotland or in England and Wales.

WHICH COURT?

Your divorce action will be heard either by the Court of Session — situated in Edinburgh — or your local sheriff court. The appropriate sheriff court for your divorce action is the one serving the area where you or your husband or wife have been living for at least 40 days before bringing the action. If you and your husband or wife have separated and live in different sheriff court areas, then you will have a choice of sheriff court.

GROUNDS FOR DIVORCE

The court will grant you a divorce if you can show that your marriage has irretrievably broken down because of:
- Your husband's or wife's adultery; OR
- Your husband or wife has behaved in such a way that you cannot reasonably be expected to live with him or her; OR
- Your husband or wife has deserted you; OR
- You have not lived with your husband or wife for at least 2 years AND he or she agrees to the divorce; OR
- You have not lived with your husband or wife for at least 5 years.

You do not have to wait for 2 years before you can get a divorce on either of the first two grounds.

ADULTERY

Your husband or wife commits adultery if he or she has sexual intercourse voluntarily with a person of the opposite sex other than you at any time during the marriage. Adultery committed after you and your husband or wife split up for some other reason is also a valid ground for divorce.

You cannot get a divorce based on any act of adultery if you condoned it. This means that you knew about it and forgave your husband or wife. If you continue or resume living together as any normal couple would for more than a 3 month period after discovering the adultery, it is assumed that you have forgiven it. But living separate lives in the same house because neither of you can find alternative accommodation does not count as forgiving.

You cannot get a divorce if you actively encourage your wife's or husband's adultery. Thus, for example, if you both take part in sex parties or similar activities, neither of you can get a divorce on the basis of your partner's adultery.

Continuing adultery is usually proved by means of private detectives who visit your husband or wife and his or her new partner. Past adultery is more difficult to prove; indirect evidence such as having shared a bedroom is acceptable.

You can divorce your husband or wife for behaving in such a way that you cannot reasonably be expected to live with him or her. This behaviour must have occurred after the date of your marriage . All kinds of behaviour can lead to a divorce whether it affects you, the children or others, such as relations. The test is whether you, as the kind of person you are, can reasonably be expected to live with your husband or wife. So the court will take into account the standard of conduct you expect from your partner in judging his or her behaviour. Unreasonable behaviour normally consists of positive acts such as assaults, threats of violence, insulting or domineering conduct or regular drunkenness. But it can also be omissions such as indifference to your husband or wife, unreasonable refusal of sexual relations, or spending so much time on your hobbies or sports that your husband or wife is excluded from your life. It may be a single act or continuing conduct. Unreasonable sexual demands, homosexuality or lesbianism may also form grounds for divorce.

You cannot complain of your husband's or wife's unreasonable behaviour if it is due to a disease, old age or an accident. For example a man who is fit and well yet spends all day in bed could find himself divorced, but a man who becomes bedridden due to a car crash could not be divorced. However, you can get a divorce if your husband's or wife's behaviour is due to insanity or mental abnormality.

BEHAVIOUR

If you are intending to sue for divorce on grounds of behaviour, you should tell people such as neighbours or relations of the incidents as they occur, so that they will be in a position to give evidence if required. Also if you become physically or mentally ill as a result of your husband's or wife's behaviour, you should see your doctor and state the cause of your illness, rather than cover up. Your doctor will then be in a position to certify, if required, that your husband's or wife's conduct has adversely affected your health. The police may be able to provide evidence if they were called after your husband or wife had assaulted you.

DESERTION

Your husband or wife deserts you if:—
- He or she voluntarily lives apart from you but you wish to live together; AND
- For a period of two years after he or she left you have continued to live apart; AND
- You have not refused a genuine and reasonable offer to live together again.

Your husband or wife must mean to leave you. If he or she is sent to prison or goes into hospital, that is not desertion. Taking up employment abroad against your wishes would be desertion if it would be unreasonable for you to accompany him or her. You cannot get a divorce for desertion if you have given your husband or wife reasonable cause for leaving you, such as your adultery or unreasonable behaviour.

The partner who deserts is usually the one who leaves the home but this is not always the case. For example, if your husband beats you and throws you out of the home, it is he who is in desertion, not you. Or if he gets a better job in another place and you refuse to join him there, you will be treated as deserting him.

If you want to use desertion as a ground for divorce you must have lived apart from your husband or wife for a total period of 2 years. But this period does not have to be unbroken, as long as the periods when you live together do not exceed 6 months. If they do a fresh 2 year period during which you live apart has to elapse.

EXAMPLE

Andrew deserted Jean on 1 January 1984. They were reconciled and lived together from 1 January to 30 April 1985 and then split up finally. Jean can start a divorce action on 1 May 1986.

But if the reconciliation lasted until 31 July 1985, no action can be taken until 1 August 1987.

NON-COHABITATION

You can get a divorce if you have not lived together with your husband or wife for a certain period. This period is 2 years if your husband or wife agrees to you bringing divorce proceedings, otherwise it is 5 years.

The reason why you are not living together does not matter. As long as your husband or wife is away — in hospital, in prison or working abroad for example — for the requisite period you can get a divorce. Living together means living as a married couple normally would. If you and your husband or wife stop sleeping together and lead separate lives in the same house, you are not living together as a normal couple.

If you and your husband or wife resume living together again for a period or periods totalling more than 6 months after the initial separation and then separate finally you must wait for another 2 or 5 years before divorce is possible. But as long as you do not live together for more than 6 months in all a fresh period is unnecessary, although you cannot count the time you have spent living together towards the 2 or 5 year period. See the example above which shows how similar rules work for the 2 year desertion period.

The court will not grant a divorce on the basis of 5 years non-cohabitation if your husband or wife would suffer grave financial hardship because of the divorce. Grave financial hardship could occur in the case of an elderly wife who would lose the chance of a widow's pension from the state or her husband's pension scheme on divorce. This financial hardship can often be compensated for by the husband taking out appropriate life insurance.

If you are divorcing your husband or wife on the basis of 2 years non-cohabitation he or she must consent to the divorce being granted. Your husband or wife is entitled to give consent on conditions, for example that you do not ask for any financial award, or that he or she will have custody of the children. The court will not interfere with these conditions; if you find them unacceptable you will have to wait a further 3 years so that you can get a divorce on the ground of 5 years non-cohabitation, or find some other ground, such as adultery. Your husband or wife can withdraw his or her consent at any time before the court grants a divorce.

DIY DIVORCE

You can get a divorce without a solicitor by using the DIY procedure (properly called the simplified procedure). You can use this procedure if the grounds of divorce are non-cohabitation for 2 or 5 years. In the case of the 2 year period your husband or wife must consent to the divorce.

Certain conditions must also apply:
- The divorce is uncontested; AND
- There are no children of the marriage under 16 years old; AND
- No financial claims are being made; AND
- There are no other proceedings affecting your marriage which have still to be heard; AND
- Neither you nor your husband or wife is suffering from mental disorder.

You can obtain the necessary forms from your local sheriff court, the Court of Session or a Citizens Advice Bureau. You will also get an easy-to-understand leaflet which tells you how to complete the forms. The basic cost is £40, but if you are on Supplementary Benefit, have a low income or are seeing a solicitor under the Legal Advice and Assistance Scheme, this fee is waived. You will have to obtain a copy of your marriage certificate if you have not already got one.

Once you have completed the forms you send them to the court (the Court of Session or your local sheriff court) which then sends a copy to your husband or wife by post. If the copy cannot be delivered by post, you will have to pay for a sheriff officer to serve the copy in another way. You can expect to obtain a divorce within 2 months of lodging the forms in court.

ORDINARY DIVORCE PROCEDURE

If you think you have grounds for divorce but you cannot use the DIY procedure, go and see a solicitor. He or she will discuss whether you have grounds, what financial orders you might apply for and whether you should apply for custody of the children.

STARTING THE ACTION

If your solicitor is satisfied that you have grounds for divorce he or she will then lodge with the court a document which sets out your claims and the evidence and arguments in support of them. This document has to be served on your husband or wife, usually by post. If you are seeking a divorce on the grounds of adultery, a copy must also be served on the person with whom you allege your husband or wife committed adultery.

In the cases of non-cohabitation for 2 or 5 years a notice is sent to your husband or wife with the document. This notice warns of the consequences of divorce on their inheritance and pension rights and contains information about the financial orders they can apply for.

Once divorce proceedings have started you can ask for various interim orders. They are called interim orders because they only last until the divorce action is heard, although some of them may be renewed then.

INTERIM ORDERS

These interim orders include:—
- interim aliment for you and/or the children (see p 16)
- interim custody of the children (see p 78) and/or an interdict against their removal from your control or out of Scotland (see p 14)
- an interim interdict prohibiting your husband or wife from assaulting or molesting you (see p 10)
- an interim exclusion order (see p 11)
- an order preventing your husband or wife disposing of his or her property in order to defeat your claim for financial provision.

Your husband or wife will normally be given an opportunity to object to your application so you should have your evidence ready to support it.

Your husband or wife can contest your action of divorce, although the vast majority are uncontested. More commonly your husband or wife will object to your claims for financial orders or custody of the children, or apply for custody and/or financial orders themselves.

CONTESTED ACTIONS

If your husband or wife contests the case, it is heard in court and you and your witnesses will have to to appear give evidence. But if only your claims for custody or financial orders are objected to, you can still use affidavit evidence (see p 92) for the divorce.

If you and your husband or wife attempt a reconciliation once the divorce proceedings are under way the court can, if asked, stop proceedings to see how it works out. If the reconciliation does not work, the fact that you and your husband lived together will not prevent you obtaining a divorce.

RECONCILIATION

AFFIDAVIT EVIDENCE

Instead of having to give evidence orally in court, you and your witnesses may be able to give evidence by means of a sworn statement called an affidavit. Generally speaking you can give evidence by affidavit unless the divorce is contested. Your solicitor will prepare the affidavit for you and the witnesses to sign, and you should make sure that the statements contained in it reflect the up-to-date position, otherwise a further affidavit will be necessary. A second affidavit would be required if the position changes after the first affidavit is lodged in court, or the court requires additional information.

CUSTODY

Before the court grants a divorce it must be satisfied that the arrangements being made for any children are satisfactory or the best that can be devised in the circumstances.

Where you and your husband or wife agree as to custody, the court usually accepts the agreed arrangements. A person who knows the children well — a grandparent or a neighbour for example — will have to give evidence of the children's circumstances and of the suitability of the proposed arrangements.

If you and your husband or wife cannot agree on future arrangements for the children, the court will require much more information to enable it to settle the dispute (see p 78).

GRANTING THE DIVORCE

Where the court is satisfied that you are entitled to a divorce and that the custody of the children is settled it will grant a divorce. It is possible to leave the financial matters outstanding to a later date, although it is normally better to have everything dealt with at the same time.

NOTIFICATION OF DIVORCE

You or your solicitor will be told when the court grants the divorce. Your husband or wife has 14 days in which to appeal in the case of a sheriff court divorce (21 days in the Court of Session). After that, if no appeal is taken, you can obtain from the court a document showing the divorce and any orders which the court made on finance, custody and other matters.

The court will inform your husband or wife of the divorce if their address is known. The Registrar General for Scotland is also informed so that the divorce can be registered.

WHAT WILL IT COST?

The expenses of any legal proceedings consist of your solicitor's fees and outlays such as postage, telephone calls and fees paid by your solicitor to others involved in the case (such as an advocate or sheriff officer). Even in an ordinary undefended divorce these can amount to £400 — £500, while the expenses of a defended divorce can easily exceed £5,000.

You can recover your expenses from your husband or wife only if he or she agreed to pay them.

The court has a complete discretion in deciding whether one person should pay their opponent's expenses as well as their own. Certain rules set out below were followed in the vast majority of cases, but practice may well change as a result of the Family Law (Scotland) Act 1985.

A wife who successfully brings a divorce or separation action based on her husbands's adultery, behaviour or desertion will generally have her expenses paid for by her husband, whether or not she is legally aided. Once her husband pays her expenses, the contribution she paid towards her legal aid will be repaid to her, although it may take years for this to happen. If the husband is legally aided, the court may not order him to pay all his wife's expenses. It will usually reduce them to what he can reasonably afford bearing in mind his income and any maintenance he has been ordered to pay. When this is done his wife will not have her contributions refunded.

A husband who successfully brings an action based on his wife's adultery, behaviour or desertion will usually have to pay his own expenses. He may also have to pay his wife's expenses as well, unless the court thinks she contested the action on frivolous grounds, or she has enough money to pay her own expenses.

The general rule for divorces granted on the grounds of non-cohabitation for 2 or 5 years is that each person pays their own expenses only. A person may, however, make it a condition of consenting to a 2 year divorce that he or she will not have to pay any expenses.

A wife who is unsuccessful in her action will have to pay her husband's expenses only if her action was frivolous or she has a substantial income or savings of her own.

DIY DIVORCES

ORDINARY DIVORCE PROCEDURE

THE LEGAL AID FUND'S CHARGE

If you are legally aided and the Legal Aid Fund fails to recover the amount it has spent on your action from your contributions (if any) and the expenses your husband or wife has been ordered to pay by the court, the Fund can recover the balance out of any sums awarded to you or property which you recover or is preserved for you as a result of your action.

This rule is unlikely to affect your divorce proceedings because it DOES NOT apply to court orders for:
- aliment whether awarded on divorce or in separate proceedings
- periodical allowance on divorce
- a lump sum on divorce
- a transfer of property on divorce
- any incidental order under section 14(2) of the Family Law (Scotland) Act 1985, for example an order for sale of the home and division of the proceeds between you and your husband or wife or an order requiring your husband or wife to return your belongings to you.

The rule WILL apply if you obtain orders such as division and sale of the home or recovery of belongings in proceedings which are separate from your divorce action.

It is possible that regulations made under the Legal Aid (Scotland) Act 1986 (planned to come into force in April 1987) may allow recovery from lump sums and transfers of property. You should check the position with your solicitor before you embark on expensive litigation.

JUDICIAL SEPARATION AND NULLITY

This chapter looks at judicial separation and nullity actions.

GETTING A JUDICIAL SEPARATION

SHOULD I GET SEPARATED OR DIVORCED?

GETTING YOUR MARRIAGE ANNULLED

GETTING A JUDICIAL SEPARATION

You can apply to the court for a judicial separation instead of a divorce. The grounds are exactly the same (see p 86). Judicial separations are rather uncommon nowadays.

The advantages of judicial separation over divorce are :—
- You remain entitled to widow's benefits or a pension from the state or your husband's pension scheme, should your husband die before you;
- You may object to divorce on religious grounds;
- Your occupancy rights in the home do not come to an end. But though they come to an end on divorce, you can apply to the divorce court to renew them after divorce (see p 50).

The disadvantages are:—
- You are still married so that you cannot remarry;
- You cannot ask the court for a capital sum or a transfer of property. You can only get aliment.

A decree of separation does not prohibit your partner from living with you or visiting you. If you want to stop your partner doing this, you must get an exclusion order (see p 28).

SHOULD I GET DIVORCED OR SEPARATED?

Any property a wife acquires after getting a judicial separation from her husband will not go to him if she dies without leaving a will. There is no equivalent rule for a husband's property.

Because the grounds for separation and divorce are the same, once you have got a decree of separation you can get a divorce later (if you want to remarry for example) without having to re-prove the facts you proved in your separation action.

GETTING YOUR MARRIAGE ANNULLED

Your marriage can be annulled because it was not valid or because of sexual impotency.

A Scottish marriage is not valid if:—
- You and your partner were under 16 at the date of the ceremony; OR
- You or your partner were already married to someone else at the date of the ceremony; OR
- You or your partner were insane at the date of the ceremony or did not consent to get married; OR
- You and your partner are too closely related to each other.

Your marriage can be annulled if either you or your partner was impotent — incapable of normal sexual intercourse — at the time of the marriage and has remained impotent thereafter. You cannot have your marriage annulled if your partner becomes impotent after the marriage. The incapacity may be due to a physical defect or psychological causes. It must be incurable, or the affected person must refuse to be treated. Psychological impotence arising after marriage may give you grounds for divorce on the basis of your partner's behaviour (see p 87).

The court has the same powers to make financial awards in nullity actions as it has in divorce actions (see p 50).

Nullity actions are rare. You should consult a solicitor if you think you have grounds for having your marriage annulled.

EFFECTS OF DIVORCE OR SEPARATION

This chapter looks at some effects of divorce or separation.

NATIONALITY AND IMMIGRATION
WELFARE BENEFITS
CHANGING NAMES

NATIONALITY AND IMMIGRATION

If you are a British citizen or a Commonwealth citizen with the right of abode in the U.K., splitting up from your husband or wife will not affect your rights to enter and live in the U.K. If you are not a British citizen or Commonwealth citizen your rights may be affected. How they may be affected is set out below.

If you were married to a British citizen, a Commonwealth citizen with right of abode or a man with 'settled' status, you will have become a settled person on your marriage. Neither subsequent separation nor divorce alters your settled status so you are entitled to stay in the U.K.

Once you are a settled person you can apply for British citizenship :
● if you are still married — after 3 years residence in the U.K.; OR
● if you are not still married — after 5 years residence in the U.K.

Once you are a British citizen your status is not affected by a subsequent separation or divorce.

If you are married to a man who has a temporary immigration status in the U.K., for example a visitor, a student, or a work permit holder, you will be expected to leave the U.K. when he does. To stay longer, you will have to qualify in your own right.

If you are married to a man who is an EEC worker (a citizen of one of the member countries of the European Community working or looking for

WIVES WHO MARRIED BEFORE 26 AUGUST 1985

work in the U.K.) you will be allowed to stay in the U.K. for as long as he does. Separation should not affect this right, but divorce will probably mean that you are expected to leave the U.K.

HUSBANDS WHO MARRIED BEFORE 26 AUGUST 1985

If you married a British citizen you would have been given permission to stay in the U.K. initially for 12 months. At the end of this period you may apply for settled status. If you separate or divorce in that 12 months your application for settled status will almost certainly be refused. Once you have been given settled status separation or divorce should not affect your right to stay in the U.K.

If you married a woman who was an EEC worker (a citizen of one of the member countries of the European Community working or looking for work in the U.K.) you will be allowed to stay in the U.K. for as long as she does. Separation should not affect this right but divorce will probably mean that you are expected to leave the U.K.

If you married any other woman, your marriage would not have affected your immigration status. You would have had to qualify in your own right to stay in the U.K.

WIVES AND HUSBANDS WHO MARRIED ON OR AFTER 26 AUGUST 1985

From this date most of the rules are the same for both husbands and wives.

If you are married to a British citizen, a Commonwealth citizen with right of abode or a person with settled status, you will be given initial permission to stay in the U.K. for 12 months. You will not be given permission to stay as a husband or wife if you are under 16, but you may qualify for entry in your own right. At the end of this period you may apply for settled status. If you separate or divorce in that 12 months your application for settled status will almost certainly be refused. Once you have been given settled status, separation or divorce should not affect your right to stay in the U.K.

If you married an EEC worker (a citizen of one of the member countries of the European Community working or looking for work in the U.K.) you will be allowed to stay in the U.K. for as long as he or she does. Separation should not affect this right but divorce will probably mean that you are expected to leave the U.K.

If you are married to a person who has been given permission to stay in the U.K. for a limited time (for instance as a student or a work permit holder) separation or divorce will mean you have to qualify in your own right if you want to stay.

If you are a cohabitee you will have to qualify for entry or staying in your own right. Splitting up has no effect on your immigration status or rights.

COHABITEES

After divorce you will not be entitled to any widow's benefits based on your ex- husband's contributions should he die subsequently. See p 60 for how divorce affects your rights under your ex-husband's or ex-wife's private pension scheme.

WELFARE BENEFITS

If you divorce before you reach retirement age (65 for a man, 60 for a woman), your state retirement pension is calculated on either your own contribution record, or your ex-husband's or ex-wife's record if that will give you a higher pension. You can only rely on his or her record as long as neither of you remarry. On your remarriage before retirement age, your future pension will be calculated on the basis of your own contributions, or those of your new husband or wife, whichever gives you a better pension. If your ex-husband or wife remarries but you don't, your pension is calculated on your contributions only. This can have a very serious effect on ex-wives' pensions.

If you divorce after retirement age, you should inform your local DHSS office at once, so that your and your ex-husband's or ex-wife's pensions can be adjusted.

Separation has no effect on your entitlement to widow's benefits or a retirement pension. But you will lose your widow's benefits if you are living with another man.

CHANGING NAMES

On splitting up a woman may wish to change back to her own name, but she is entitled to continue using her (ex)husband's name if she wants to.

A mother may want to change her children's surnames to that of her new husband when she remarries. You should think carefully before you do this. It may make things easier for you, your husband and the children to have the same surname in that your divorce is concealed. On the other hand, the children's father (and perhaps the children too) may resent a change. Nowadays, with so many marriages breaking up, it has ceased to be embarrassing for children to have different names from the adults looking after them.

You can change your and the children's names simply by telling everyone concerned (employer, doctor, school, etc.) of the new name. Personal documents such as child benefit books and passports will have to be altered. A change in the children's names can be registered in an official register — the Register of Corrections Etc. — if the children were born in Scotland. The advantage of official registration is that a new birth certificate can be obtained showing their new names. To register a change you should see your local Registrar of Births, Deaths and Marriages. If the children's father was married to you, he must agree to any change and sign the appropriate forms.

LEGAL AID

You can be helped to pay for legal services if you cannot afford to pay a solicitor yourself. There are three different schemes: the fixed fee interview scheme, legal advice and assistance, and legal aid. Most solicitors undertake legal aid work. A list of those who do can be obtained from your local Legal Aid Committee (the address is in the phone book), Citizens Advice Bureau or Sheriff Court.

The amounts of money mentioned below change fairly frequently. They were correct as at the date of writing this book, but will give a rough guide only as to the position in the future.

FIXED FEE INTERVIEW SCHEME

Many solicitors are prepared to give an interview of up to half an hour for not more than £5. In this way you can get preliminary advice at low cost on your difficulties, even if you would not qualify for legal advice and assistance or legal aid. Solicitors taking part in this scheme are listed in the Legal Aid Referral List or the Law Society's Directory of General Services (see Appendix 3).

LEGAL ADVICE AND ASSISTANCE

Under this scheme (sometimes called the pink form scheme) you can receive up to £50 worth of legal help, although more may be authorised if an application is made by your solicitor for an increase. Almost any kind of help on matters the Scottish courts can deal with may be provided, such as advising on your rights to aliment, occupancy of the house or an inheritance. Your solicitor can also do conveyancing or the preparation of agreements relating to your home under the scheme. Court or tribunal appearances are not covered although your solicitor can help you to present your case yourself. Legal advice and assistance is also useful for getting preliminary advice and paying for initial investigations to see whether you have a good case for which legal aid could be obtained to begin court proceedings.

Legal advice and assistance is free if your savings (excluding your home and contents) are less than £800 and your net income (after tax, and national insurance contributions) is below £54 per week. If your net income is more than £114 per week you will not get any help under the scheme. In between £54 and £114 you have to pay a proportion of the cost according to a sliding scale. All these figures are increased if you have dependants living with you.

Your spouse's or cohabiting partner's income is added to yours in order to see whether you qualify for legal advice and assistance. But this rule does not apply if you are claiming against your husband, wife or partner or defending a claim made by him or her, or if you are living apart.

If, as a result of the legal advice and assistance given, you succeed in your claim or successfully resist a claim against your property, the cost of the advice and assistance given may be deducted from the value of your claim or property. But no deduction is made from aliment awarded to you.

LEGAL AID

Under this scheme you can get help with the expenses of legal proceedings before the courts. Examples where legal aid may be available include proceedings for divorce, separation, maintenance, occupancy rights or an interdict against violence. The scheme does not cover matters such as house purchase or advice relating to tax or benefits since you are not making or defending a claim.

In order to get legal aid
- the appropriate legal aid committee must be satisfied that you have a reasonable case. Your solicitor may need to do some work beforehand investigating and getting evidence for your claim. You can get help with the cost of the preliminary work by means of the legal advice and assistance scheme, as legal aid generally only helps with expenses incurred after you have been granted legal aid. AND
- your income and savings are below certain limits (which are increased if you have dependants living with you). Your spouse or cohabiting partner's income and savings will be counted in, unless you are claiming against your husband, wife or partner, or defending a claim by him or her, or if you are living apart. As a rough guide to present limits a married couple with 2 children would qualify for some legal aid if their income was less than £250 per week gross, while if they earned less than £150 per week gross they would get free legal aid. In between these figures you will have to pay a proportion of the cost according to a sliding scale. The corresponding limits for savings are £4710 to £3000. Your house and contents are not counted as savings but life policies and business interests are included.

If you are successful in your claim your opponent normally has to pay your expenses, but see p 93 for the rules on divorce expenses. Where the Legal Aid Fund recovers these expenses in full from your opponent, you will have any contributions you paid towards your legal aid refunded. A refund may, however, take a long time to be paid. If the Legal Aid Fund fails to recover these expenses from your opponent, it is entitled to deduct them from the amount the court has awarded you, or property which has been preserved or recovered for you as a result of your proceedings. This rule does not apply to orders made on divorce or any aliment (see p|94|). Where the claim for which legal aid was granted involved the home the Legal Aid Fund may take a security over it for unrecovered expenses. This means that when the home is sold you will have to pay these expenses out of the price you get.

If you lose your case the normal rule is that you have to pay your opponent's expenses as well as your own, but see p 93 for the rules on divorce expenses. The court will not normally order you to pay your opponent's expenses if you are legally aided. If you are ordered to pay and your opponent is legally aided, the Legal Aid Fund will ask you for further contributions, over and above those you have already paid. If your opponent is not legally aided and you are ordered to pay his or her expenses, then his or her solicitor will ask you for payment.

THE MEANING OF SOME LEGAL TERMS YOU MAY COME ACROSS

ADVOCATE	A person who pleads or conducts a case in court.
AFFIDAVIT	A document containing a sworn statement which can be used in evidence. This avoids a personal appearance in court.
ALIMENT	Money paid to a spouse or child for their support — maintenance.
BANKRUPT	Insolvent. A bankrupt's whole property is made over by the court to a trustee in order that the trustee may sell it to pay the bankrupt's debts.
CHILDREN'S HEARING/PANEL	A tribunal consisting of 3 lay people who decide how to deal with children who have committed offences or who are in need of care.
CUSTODY	The right of an adult (usually a parent) to care for and control a child.
DECREE	An order of a court.
DEFENDER	The person who contests or defends a court action.
DEFENCES	The document lodged in court in which the defender sets out the facts and arguments contesting the pursuer's claim.
DOMICILE	The country where the law considers a person's permanent residence to be, or with which the person has most connections.
EXCLUSION ORDER	A court order suspending a person's right to occupy the family home.
EXPENSES	The fees, outlays and other sums payable by a person involved in court action to the solicitors, advocates, court officials and other concerned in the action.

An English term with no clear meaning in Scotland. One meaning is a person entitled to represent a child in legal proceedings or to look after his property.	GUARDIAN
Non-moveable property, mainly land and buildings.	HERITABLE PROPERTY (HERITAGE)
The document which sets out the pursuer's case in the sheriff court (except summary causes). Service of this on the defender starts the proceedings.	INITIAL WRIT
A court order prohibiting a person from doing the act(s) specified in the order.	INTERDICT
An order pronounced by a court pending final disposal of the case. Thus interim interdict, interim exclusion order and so on.	INTERIM ORDER
Rights of inheritance which can be claimed by a husband, wife or children even where there is a will.	LEGAL RIGHTS
A popular term used to refer to aliment and periodical allowance.	MAINTENANCE
Goods capable of being moved, money in cash or in accounts and "paper rights" like shares and insurance policies.	MOVEABLE PROPERTY (MOVEABLES)
The rights to live in, occupy and return to a home.	OCCUPANCY RIGHTS
A weekly or monthly sum of money ordered by the court on granting divorce to be paid by one spouse to the other.	PERIODICAL ALLOWANCE
The hearing of evidence in a court action. Diet of proof — the date when evidence is to be heard.	PROOF
The person who makes a claim in a court action.	PURSUER
A person who serves documents and enforces orders of the sheriff court. The equivalent for the Court of Session is a messenger-at-arms.	SHERIFF OFFICER
The document which sets out the pursuer's case in the Court of Session or in summary causes in the sheriff court.	SUMMONS
A document in which a person states how his or her property is to be disposed of after death.	WILL

GOING TO A SOLICITOR

Most solicitors in Scotland handle problems arising out of splitting up. You may already have a "family lawyer" who has acted for you before, but you may not want to consult him or her in connection with proceedings against your partner. Your friends may be able to recommend a solicitor.

HOW DO I FIND A SOLICITOR?

The local library may hold copies of the Legal Aid Solicitors Referral List or the Law Society of Scotland's Directory of General Services. These provide information on solicitors and what types of work they are prepared to handle. A solicitor can usually be found by looking for a Legal Aid sign displayed outside the office, or by consulting "solicitors" in the yellow pages. However, more accurate information on the choice of solicitor available can be obtained by consulting either the local Legal Aid Secretary (under "Legal Aid" in the telephone directory) or a Citizens Advice Bureau, both of whom carry information on what types of work local solicitors are prepared to undertake and whether or not they handle legal aid work.

MAKING CONTACT

It is advisable to call or telephone the solicitors's office beforehand and ask for an appointment to see him or her, explaining briefly what your problem is about. All relevant papers should be taken to the first meeting with the solicitor.

PAYING FOR A SOLICITOR

Unless you qualify for assistance under the various legal aid schemes (see Appendix 1) you will be sent a bill in due course for the advice or action taken by the solicitor on your behalf. It is advisable to enquire about the cost at an early stage. Do not hesitate to ask the solicitor at the first interview roughly how long the work is likely to take and how much it is likely to cost. You may even want to seek quotes from several firms before selecting a solicitor to act for you. If at any stage you want a clearer idea of how the work being done by the solicitor is progressing and what it is likely to cost, follow up verbal questions with a letter (keeping a copy).

BOOKS YOU MAY FIND HELPFUL

Divorce and Your Children, Ann Hooper, pub. Unwin.

Coping with Separation and Divorce, Ann Mitchell, pub. Chambers.

Bringing up Children on your own, Liz McNeill Taylor, pub. Fontana.

Getting Free, Ginny Nicarthy, pub. Seal Express.

Making the Break, Melanie Caren Jones and Hester Watson, pub. Pelican.

Learning to Live Without Violence — a Handbook for Men, Daniel Sankin and Michael Durphy, pub. Volcano Press.

BOOKS FOR THE CHILDREN

I Have Two Homes, Althea, pub. Dinosaur.

Divorce : The Child's Point of View, Yvette Walczak with Shiela Burns, pub. Harper and Row.

Printed in Scotland by Holmes McDougall Ltd., Edinburgh.